THE GREATEST OF THESE

A 90 DAY DEVOTIONAL INTENDED TO HELP YOU GROW IN YOUR FAITH, HOPE AND LOVE

Janet Scott

The Greatest of These
*A 90 Day Devotional intended to help you
grow in your Faith, Hope and Love*

ISBN: 978-0-578-51628-8

This book is dedicated to my amazing parents
Eugene Dale McConnell and Ellen Irene McConnell,
who did their best to give us a godly heritage
that they had not known growing up!
They loved beyond measure both
their children and their grandchildren!
I don't know where I would be today
if it weren't for their love and prayers!

ACKNOWLEDGMENTS

My children and grandchildren have been tremendous inspiration and I love them more than life itself and have learned so much from all of them! They are truly some of my greatest blessings from the Lord!

I am overwhelmingly grateful to my husband Bill Scott for his help and support with Chocolate and God. I had gone to him one day while we were doing youth ministry to ask him to pray about the fact that I felt I was supposed to write devotions for women and the next thing I knew he had come up with a name for it (Chocolate and God) and had me ready to go! He has put in countless hours recording and producing the radio feature which is aired on several stations in the U.S. and is now being translated and used in other countries as well. He helped get this ball rolling!

My sister Jean has been a tremendous encouragement to keep pressing on through all of the struggles in my life. She has spent many hours listening, talking and laughing with me to help keep me focused on God. Her encouragement has helped me keep on keeping on!

I am grateful also to Rainer publishing for their support through this process of publishing my first book!

FOREWORD

I don't know about you, but in today's world, it seems we are busier than ever. Even with gadgets and tools that should help us accomplish everything we need to get done, the hours tick past and at the end of the day, the unchecked items on my to-do list still nag at me. And I realize something. I've been so busy *doing*, I've not spent any time *listening*. I'm not saying that what I'm doing isn't important, but some days, I forget to do *the most important* thing that can be done during the day. And that's spending time with the Lord. My Savior. The One who formed me, created me, loved me. My Abba who wants to spend time with me, whispering to my heart the things that I need for the day. For life.

Unfortunately, I'm sure I'm not the only one. My friend, Janet, has opened up her heart and allowed the Lord to breathe truths and wisdom into her spirit. Then she has turned around and written those truths into devotionals so she can share what she's learned. I don't know about you, but I'm all about letting others share what God has taught them—especially when I know that someone knows what she's talking about! I've known Janet for many years and I cherish her friendship, her humble heart and her desire to know God on the most intimate level so that she can discern his still, small voice—and obey. I want that, too! While reading Janet's devotionals, I could hear God speaking through her words, drawing me nearer to him in that precious way that He has. I encourage you, before you read this book that you would pray and ask God to speak to you, to reveal Himself to you on each page, and to bring to mind how you can apply each lesson to bring glory to Him.

God Bless you,

Lynette Eason, best-selling, award-winning author

CONTENTS

INTRODUCTION

As you flip through the pages of this devotional, you may notice that there are journaling pages and I want to make it very clear here in the beginning that those pages are there to bless, not to burden. Don't feel like you absolutely have to write something on any page, use those pages to write when you feel God is speaking to you about something or when you have a thought or memory that brings new light to the message. You may write on all of them or a few or you may not want to write anything at all and that is perfectly ok.

I have always longed for more faith! As a child, I can remember looking at the hill out beyond our fields on our little farm one day and focusing on and trying to get it to move! I took the verses literally about moving mountains if you just had the faith the size of a mustard seed. I have to admit I was a bit discouraged for a few years after that, thinking that I must not have had any faith at all since I couldn't even move a small hill! I was greatly disturbed that it didn't move an inch!

As I grew in my faith and maturity, I realized that there were many mountains in my life that needed moving and the only one who could move them was God. I began to understand that there was a lot more to faith than wanting to move a hill for no apparent reason! There's more to faith than just sitting down and trying to somehow magically move things or beg God until He sees things our way and does what we think He should do! There's a relationship, there's a walk of learning to trust and it is all within your reach but you must take the time to get to know Him. Learn about His love for you! Seek Him with your whole heart so He can fill you with His Hope and your faith will follow!

I was reading a post on Facebook last night of a woman who lost her child just shortly before her due date. She didn't just lose her child that day, she lost her faith in God. At first, I was frustrated, but then the thought struck me that we all have losses we face in life and they affect us all differently, and I have no idea all the pain she has faced. Her anger and heartache had overwhelmed her to the point that she has questioned her faith in God, unfortunately, that can happen to anyone if we don't have a deep understanding of His love for us. Satan loves to compound our heartache by feeding us the lie that God doesn't care and couldn't possibly love us or maybe even exist if He allows heartaches in our lives. None of us are above succumbing to his lies if we aren't on guard. My heart is overwhelmed and broken for this young woman and part of the reason may be simply knowing that the loss of a child must be one of the greatest losses we can possibly experience on earth, I just pray that she will find her way back to God. If Satan could possibly have a favorite mode of attack, I would tend to believe that it could be attacking our belief in His love for us!

So, with all of that said, I thought it might be good to explain here why it may seem that we have these devotions backward. We are starting with 30 days focusing on Love and then 30 on Hope and then 30 on Faith. When I sat down and started putting this together I had arranged it by Faith, Hope and then, of course, Love and then I felt God prompting me to turn it around, Love, Hope, and Faith. He really impressed on my heart that if we can somehow grasp a glimpse of His love for us, then our Hope will build and we will grow in Faith. One of my favorite quotes is by Chad Witmeyer,

"Hope never dies where faith is strong, and faith grows strong in the presence of hope." Let's face it our hope in life stems from the knowledge of God's love for us, so that is where we need to begin.

This book is designed for you to be able to write your daily thoughts and applications for your life. Don't stress over it though, there may be days you have a lot to write and you may need to have a journaling tablet to be able to hold it all, and there may be other days that you just don't feel like writing a single word. That's ok! All I ask is that you open your heart and mind up to God speaking to you to draw you closer to Him. If you find yourself just reading and you never write a word, that's ok. Use this time and material to grow in your walk with God, however, you feel led!

Before we get started in our daily devotions we first need to cover God's ultimate act of love for us. I am covering this here because none of the rest of this will matter if you have never accepted Him as your Savior.

JOHN 3:16
For God so loved the world, that He gave His only begotten son, that whosoever believeth in Him, should not perish but have everlasting life.

Don't allow your pride to keep you out of heaven! Salvation on our side of things is so simple that I think there are those who think it is too simple and too good to be true, so there must be "work" that needs to be done in order to be forgiven. I have even heard some of the most ridiculous ideas given out like the idea of needing a certain translation of the Bible in order to be saved. Seriously? That would mean Jesus lied to the thief on the cross when He told Him that "today, you will be with me in paradise." Let's not make salvation something that it isn't. God made the world and Satan has done everything He can to destroy it and the people God created in His own image. Satan is the father of lies and will do whatever He can to keep people from believing, right down to making salvation and belief in God seem too simple!

I remember accepting Jesus as my Savior when I was really little. I remember it like it was yesterday! If you have never taken the time to do that I would encourage you not to wait another moment! Don't allow pride or anything else to stand in your way! Maybe everyone around you thinks you are already saved and yet you know that there really never was a time when you gave your life to God, you have just behaved the way you were raised and used all the key phrases that Christians use because they are so common to you. Would you really want to allow your pride keep you out of heaven? Is your pride worth eternity? We so often forget how short life here on earth is and yet we are created to live for eternity! Where are you going to choose to spend it?

What about the people you love? Can you bear the thought of their going through life never accepting Christ as their Savior and knowing for all of eternity they missed heaven? I had a relative say one time to me, "do you really think a loving God would create a hell for people? If your child were bad would you throw them into a fire?" The answer to that is: God created Hell for Satan and his angels that chose to follow him and as far as throwing a child into a fire? No, of course, we wouldn't do that any more than God would, but if you told your child to stay away from the fire and you showed them the way out of a burning building and they chose to go their own way which led them straight into the fire, what then? God has made His way very clear, Hell is a choice made by individuals!

The Answer:

1 John 5:11-12 And this is the testimony: God has given us eternal life, and this life is in his Son. The one who has the Son has this eternal life; the one who does not have the Son of God does not have this eternal life.

This passage tells us that God has given us eternal life and this life is in His Son, Jesus Christ. In other words, the way to possess eternal life is to possess God's Son. The question is, how can a person have the Son of God?

Romans 5:8 But God demonstrates his own love for us, in that while we were still sinners, Christ died for us.

According to Romans 5:8, God demonstrated His love for us through the death of His Son. Why did Christ have to die for us? Because Scripture declares all men to be sinful. To "sin" means to disobey God. The Bible declares "all have sinned and fall short of the glory (the perfect holiness) of God" (Rom. 3:23). In other words, our sin separates us from God who is perfect holiness (righteousness and justice) and God must therefore judge us and our sin.

Scripture also teaches that no amount of human goodness, human works, human morality, or religious activity can gain acceptance with God or get anyone into heaven. Romans 3:10, tells us "there is none righteous, not even one". Added to this are the declarations of the following verses of Scripture:

Ephesians 2:8-9 For by grace you are saved through faith, and this is not of yourselves, it is the gift of God; 9 it is not of works, so that no one can boast.

Romans 5:8 But God demonstrates his own love for us, in that while we were still sinners, Christ died for us.

This is the good news of the Bible, the message of the gospel. It's the message of the gift of God's own Son who became man (the God-man), lived a sinless life, died on the cross for our sin, and was raised from the grave proving both the fact He is God's Son and the value of His death for us as our substitute.

How Do We Receive God's Son as our savior?

Because of what Jesus Christ accomplished for us on the cross, the Bible states "He that has the Son has life." We can receive the Son, Jesus Christ, as our Savior by personal faith, by trusting in the person of Christ and His death for our sins.

John 1:12 But to all who have received him–those who believe in his name–he has given the right to become God's children

John 3:16-18 For this is the way God loved the world: he gave his one and only Son that everyone who believes in him should not perish but have eternal life. 17 For God did not send his Son into the world to condemn the world, but that the world should be saved through him. 18 The one who believes in Him is not condemned. The one who does not believe has been condemned already, because he has not believed in the name of the one and only Son of God.

This means we must each come to God the same way: (1) as a sinner who recognizes his sinfulness, (2) realizes no human works can result in salvation, and (3) relies totally on Christ alone by faith alone for our salvation.

If you would like to receive and trust Christ as your personal Savior, take the time for a simple prayer acknowledging your sinfulness, accepting His forgiveness and putting your faith in Christ for your salvation. If you have done that, tell someone who can also help guide you into a close relationship with God. If you aren't sure who to tell please either message me on my blog or email me at janet@chocolateandgod.com , I would love to know! I would also encourage you to find a good local, Bible believing church where you can get plugged in and develop your walk with God!

Okay, so now, whether you are looking for more Faith or are desperate for some glimmer of Hope or looking for Love in all the wrong places my prayer is that as you spend the next 90 days reading through these devotions that you will be empowered by God to walk in His love, hope and faith to be all that He has created you to be! What are we waiting for? Let's dig in!

1 Corinthians 13:13, "So now faith, hope and love abide, these three; but the greatest of these is love."

WHY WOULD HE CARE

PSALM 8:4

What is man that you are mindful of him,
and the son of man, that you care for him? (ESV)

This is a real question that I know we have all had at least one time or another! I was asking God this morning about this very thing: Why would you (God of All) care about the details of my life? There are so many people out there, why would my frustrations, struggles, wounded heart, joys sorrows, desires and path for my life matter, I am just a smudge on a map when you look at it all. How is it possible that you really care about just one little person and every detail of their life?

We all toss around the statements that have been familiar since early childhood or from when you first accepted Him as your Savior about God's love for us that are meant to comfort and encourage. I feel as though the real impact and meaning of those words often have been lost due to our experiences with the selfishness of the "human heart". The words, I love you, are sometimes spoken by people that you know don't have an ounce of love for you or they say that they love you and turn around and break your heart into a million pieces. Where's the love?

This morning as I was praying and just admiring how amazing God is, that was my question: as Big and awesome and wonderful as you are, why would you be concerned about the details of one little person like me? The answer is actually pretty simple: When I was pregnant with my 2nd child, I remember wondering how I could possibly have room in my heart to love this child as much as I did my first one. When I had my 3rd child, it wasn't even a question because I realized that it wouldn't matter how many children I had there would always be more love and room in my heart for that one too! God is capable of so much more than we could ever think and He is able to love beyond even the love of a Mom. No matter how many people there have ever been or how many there ever will be, God loves you and He cares about every detail of your life just as much as He ever has about anyone else or ever will in the future! This isn't a passive love or a flippant, meaningless comment ~ You mean more to Him than words can explain! He loves you more than anyone ever has or ever will! You are precious in His eyes and what you are facing today is important to Him, whether you are on the Mountaintop or you are in the depths of a valley that is overwhelming your heart ~ He is there and He cares! You are as important as Esther or Hannah or Mary or David or Job, ... you matter to Him.

So with this in mind, today ~ trust Him, pour your heart out to Him, run to His throne with a new boldness and understanding of just how much He loves and cares for you! Hold on to that truth today! Truly, the best is yet to come!

Quote:

"All that we love deeply becomes a part of us."
HELEN KELLER

~ How Can You Apply This to Your Life Today?~

~ DAY 2 ~

THE LOVE IN HIS EYES

2 CHRONICLES 16:9A
For the eyes of the Lord run to and fro throughout the whole earth, to give strong support to those whose heart is blameless toward him. (ESV)

Where can you find answers? Where can you find the love of God? Where can you find hope and strength for your day? In His eyes! The answers, His love, your hope, strength, peace and all that you may need will only be found in His eyes.

Seek Him with your whole heart! Life is going to be a struggle, that is very clear, but you can find hope, you can find love and strength. Psalm 121: 1-3, "I lift up my eyes to the hills. From where does my help come? My help comes from the Lord, who made heaven and earth. He will not let your foot be moved; He who keeps you will not slumber." (ESV) God is always watching, His eyes are on you, will you lift your eyes up to see His answer. Ask Him today what His vision is for your life.

We live in an imperfect world and there are going to be storms in life and overwhelming struggles that can leave you wondering. Hold on to Him! Seek Him! Don't look for answers anywhere else.

As long as you live in this world, satan is going to everything he can to tear you away from God. It is your choice, will you follow God and cling to Him through it all or are you going to allow satan to pull you away so he can have you to himself. If satan can get you to believe that the struggles in your life and the heartache and pain are God's fault instead of satan's or yours, then he can separate you to devour you. 1 Peter 5:8 tells us, "Be sober-minded; be watchful. Your adversary the devil prowls around like a roaring lion, seeking someone to devour." (ESV) He is always trying to separate and divide so he can devour. Don't buy the lies! God loves you and wants to see you through everything you are facing in life!

Seek His eyes! Ask Him to show you His answers for your life! Ask Him for His strength and protection for the day! Hold on to His truth, found only in His word! God is faithful! It is ok to have questions and to wonder why or what on earth...... but don't buy satan's lies! Seek God, knowing that you can trust Him! Know that He cares for you beyond anything you could possibly understand! Give it all to Him! Hold on to Jeremiah 29:11, "For I know the plans I have for you," declares the Lord, "plans to prosper you and not to harm you, plans to give you hope and a future." (NIV)

Quote:

"Whether you think you can, or think you can't...... you're right."
HENRY FORD

~ How Can You Apply This To Your Life Today ~

~ DAY 3 ~

ALLOW HIM TO FILL YOU WITH HIS LOVE

EPHESIANS 5:1-2
Be ye therefore followers of God, as dear children;
And walk in love, as Christ also hath loved us,
and hath given himself for us an offering
and a sacrifice to God for a sweet-smelling savor. (KJV)

You are not always necessarily going to "feel" like showing love to some people, but according to these verses, you are to do it anyhow. You cannot base what you do on how you feel. Your feelings will always tend to lead you down a wrong path because you are human, you need to imitate God! Ask Him for His love when you aren't "feeling it"! You need to guide your feelings and check them at the door of your mind, you just can't base what you say and do strictly on how you feel. Feelings are like a two year old; you don't want them driving your car but you aren't going to put them in the trunk either! Find a godly balance!

If you ask God to fill you with His love and ask Him to help you walk in it, you will be amazed at how much easier it is to love people!

Ladies, this is really something that needs to happen more between us! The "cat fights" need to stop! You don't have to be jealous of what she looks like, what she does or says! There isn't a woman on earth who has anything over you if you are following God and doing what He has called you to! We are called to love each other! Satan loves to pit women against women because he knows if we come together we are a force to be reckoned with. No more! Let's start coming together to fight this battle together! Don't you dare flirt with someone else's husband! If another woman's husband has the nerve to flirt with you, put that man in his place! If he would cheat on her, he will cheat on you! There is nothing flattering about a man who will flirt with you at the expense of the woman he is with! Remember Eleanor Roosevelt's saying: "No one can make you feel inferior without your consent!" Let's start praying for more love for each other! Let's make sure we have each other's backs!

The world is starving for love! Let's all pursue showing more of God's love to all those around us! Ask God to show you even little things that you can do that will show His love for them! Trust me, it won't hurt you to reach out in love to others, it will actually bless you beyond what you can imagine! Ask Him today to fill you with His love for people so that they can see that in Him, the best is yet to come for them as well!

Quote:

"Graciousness is more than good manners.
It is more than courtesy. It is the etiquette of the soul.
True graciousness has such a divine quality we feel it is
something that comes through us and not from us."
FRED SMITH

~ How Can You Apply This to Your Life Today? ~

~ DAY 4 ~

HOW TO LOVE AS HE LOVES

LUKE 6:28
*Bless them that curse you, and pray for
them which despitefully use you.*

God's love toward others should be so evident in our lives and yet there are times and seasons in our lives when that can seem to be a true challenge! Where does the love come from, how can you keep it and how do you show it to those that are just set on driving you insane?

One of you asked me the other day, how do we love someone who hates us?! It brought back the memory of someone asking me that a few years ago....... When Bill's Mom was diagnosed with cancer it was a shock to all of us! She was a juicer and she took vitamins and we seriously thought she may out live us all! When she was diagnosed she said she wanted me to be her caregiver if things didn't work out for the best. She wanted to stay home, home was the Mother in-law suite attached to our home. Now, you have to understand that Bill was her favorite child, so there was always a bit of tension between us because she used to tell me that I was in her way.

It was hard for her to let go of her "boy". As a mom, I get that, we all handle our children moving on and leaving differently. As she began going through all the stages one goes through with cancer; denial, anger and frustration, it was tough because she went through it all! At first I wondered how we were going to survive and how was I going to be able to handle all that was coming! I finally got to the point where I prayed every single time I walked over there and throughout my day that God would help me to treat her as though she were Him! I kept running through my mind, over and over, "how would I want my mom to be treated?" Then one day a lady that stopped by to see her and she asked me, "how can you be nice to someone who is so mean to you?"

You don't answer to God for how someone else treats you, but you will stand before God and answer for how you treat them! You aren't going to change hateful people by acting like them! The only thing that will change anyone is the love of God! We are called to treat others in a way that pleases Him and there are times in life when that is the only thing that will drive you to do it! Matthew 25:45 tells us, Then he will answer them, saying, "Truly, I say to you, as you did not do it to one of the least of these, you did not do it to me." (ESV) Trust me, I have had much more difficult people in my life than Bill's Mom and she was ill, but no matter who it is or what they may be going through, the answer is still the same. Pray, pray, pray! Ask God to give you His love for them and the strength to be who you need to be in spite of all they are saying or doing. They don't have to be your best friend and you don't have to have them over for dinner. You are just called to respond with the love of Christ and believe me there will be many times that the only way to do that is with God holding your hand with one of his, and if you are like me, there are times I have to have Him hold His other hand over my mouth!

Quote:

*"If what you believe doesn't affect
how you live, then it isn't very important."*
DICK NOGLEBERG

~ How Can You Apply This to Your Life Today ~

~ DAY 5 ~

THE BEST DAD EVER

PSALM 46:1
God is our refuge and strength,
a very present help in trouble. (KJV)

How do you see God? Is He brutal? Is He just waiting for you to do something wrong so He can pounce on it and discipline you? Do you see Him as distant, not really caring what goes on in your life because you feel insignificant? Or, do you see Him as a loving, caring God who sees and hears and is by your side, walking through life with you, wanting to be a part of every detail, just like a loving, protecting and uplifting God?

We all know that a lot of our outlook on God can come from our opinion of our relationship with our Dad and that can either make our walk with Him closer or very distant if we allow it to. That thought process can be very difficult to overcome, if you aren't aware that is what is holding you back. My children always felt as though their Dad was very distant in their lives, but let me tell you what; they had a very active Papa (Grandpa)! When we lost my Dad, the loss to me and my children was overwhelming and devastating! To them, they lost the only really close loving 'father figure' they had and of course to me he was my Dad. As a old friend of mine once put it, "it wasn't just that we had lost someone we loved so much, it was that we lost someone who loved us that much!" My point here is this: maybe you weren't close to your Dad and maybe you weren't able to have a loving grandfather(hopefully you did), but God still loves you that much! He wants more than ever to fill that role in your life! Don't push Him away, He wants to show you that kind of love! He wants you to draw close to Him so He can be your refuge and strength! He never intended for you to face life alone! He wants to face each and every day with you, experiencing your joys and to carry you through your sorrows! He loves you more than humanly possible!

No matter what you are facing today, turn to Him! Give Him everything that is weighing you down today and allow Him to be your refuge and strength. Don't go it alone! Let Him wrap His arms around you today and carry you through to the other side! The best is yet to come!

Quote:

"Courage doesn't always roar; sometimes it is that quiet voice at the end of the day saying, 'I will try again tomorrow'"
SIMPLE TRUTHS

~ How Can You Apply This To Your Life Today ~

~ DAY 6 ~

EVEN A SPARROW CAN HAVE A BAD DAY

LUKE 12:6-7

Are not five sparrows sold for two pennies, and not one of them is forgotten before God? Why even the very hairs of your head are all numbered. Fear not you are of more value than many sparrows. (ESV)

We serve such a mighty God that He knows and cares when even a sparrow is having a bad day, how much more will He care about yours? As it says in verse 27 of this chapter; "Consider the lilies, how they grow: they neither toil nor spin, yet I tell you that even Solomon in all of his glory was not arrayed like one of these." (ESV) Ladies, I think maybe we all worry too much about whether or not we are going to be cared for by God especially when we are asked to step out in faith for something. God cares about every detail of our lives.

I really think that there are many times when the reason I am "lacking" in an area is because I haven't taken the time to pray about it. I know that God knows what we need even before we ask or think about it but He still wants to hear from you! He wants to be sought out, He wants us to want a genuine relationship with him not just see Him as the "Quick Order Catalog" in the sky! Jeremiah 29:12-13 says, "Then you will call upon me and come and pray to me, and I will hear you. You will seek me and find me, when you seek me with all your heart." This doesn't mean that you take inventory of what your needs are and make a list and sit down and pour it all out before God and then you are off and running again, it means He wants you to truly seek Him

God doesn't want some wishy washy relationship where you just show up because you need something, He wants you to seek Him with your whole heart! He wants your love and attention, He wants you to get to know Him. He loves you that much! James 1:6-7 says, "But let him ask in faith, with no doubting, for the one who doubts is like a wave of the sea that is driven and tossed by the wind. For that person must not suppose that at the will receive anything from the Lord;" When we get to know Him we will have the faith we need to understand that He will do what is best when we ask Him for something and when we truly seek to know Him we will ask in faith and with the right attitudes and motives.

It amazes me when I think of how vast the world is and that God knows everything about every little thing! Nothing escapes His notice. We think we are doing well when we multi-task, I would say our multi-tasking doesn't even scratch the surface of it. God is God and we need to be sure that we don't limit Him by what we are capable of or by what we comprehend. We cannot comprehend all that He is and all that He does so we just have to trust that nothing is too difficult for Him and He has a plan because He hasn't missed a thing that has gone on or will go on. Trust Him today to meet you where you are and to meet your every need. Seek Him with your whole heart, don't settle for an acquaintance relationship with Him, really get to know Him! He wants to pour out His love on you, that love you have been waiting for all your life! The best is yet to come!

Quote:

"Nothing great was ever accomplished without enthusiasm."
RALPH WALDO EMERSON

~ How Can You Apply This To Your Life Today ~

~ DAY 7 ~

HIS LOVE COVERS IT ALL

LUKE 15:21-24

And the son said to him, Father, I have sinned against heaven, and before you. I am no longer worthy to be called your son. Bu the father said to his servants, 'Brig quickly the best robe, and put it on him, and put a ring on his hand, and shoes on his feet. And bring the fattened calf and kill it, and let us eat and celebrate. For this my son was dead, and is alive again; he was lost, and is found.' And they began to celebrate. (ESV)

I know this is such a familiar story to most, but it is a very important parable! Have any of you had a time or times in your life when you lived in rebellion? I know I have. I can look back and wonder what I was thinking when I was younger and if I allow him to Satan just loves to beat me up over every little detail.

Jesus told this parable for that very reason! Satan wants to keep you from being all you can be by making you feel like you aren't worthy to be anything for God. If you have something from your past that you have repented of and have asked for God's forgiveness, recognize His response; "bring quickly the best robe and put it on her and put a ring on her hand and shoes on her feet (in other words, clothe her from head to toe as my child, not as the least of my children but with the best of my attire!) and bring out the best calf and kill it so we can have a celebration that she is back!" He doesn't expect you to "pay" for it for a while..... there are always natural consequences to sin, but He will carry you through those too.... Jesus already paid for your sin! God loves you so much He is just glad to have you back and now He wants to use you to be all He created you to be if you will just allow Him to! Celebrate with Him for the future He has and don't allow Satan to imprison you with your past!

Now I know that there are many of you who haven't wasted days, or months or years living in rebellion and that is absolutely fantastic and believe me God rejoices over you and your unfailing commitment to Him, every day! You have been a true blessing to His heart! I would encourage you to rejoice with Him and join in the celebration when you see someone who turns their life around. Don't be like this man's other son in this parable, who had a fit. Verses 28-31, But he was angry and refused to go in. His father came out and entreated him but he answered his father, "Look, these many years I have served you, and I never disobeyed your command, yet you never gave me a young goat, that I might celebrate with my friends,. But when this son of yours came who has devoured your property with prostitutes, you killed the fattened calf for him!" And he said to him, "son, you are always with me, and all that is mine is yours. It was fitting to celebrate and be glad, for this your brother was dead, and is alive; he was lost and is found." (ESV) Don't snub those that God has brought back to Him. Don't allow Satan to tell you that they shouldn't be allowed in your "elite" group! Be a mentor, help them get back on their feet so they can better serve God! God wants to use you to help get them back on the right track. Our goal here ladies is to all reach a place of serving Him better and it takes all of us helping each other! You may be surprised as you mentor how much you will learn from their experience!

Quote:

"No one can make you feel inferior without your consent."
ELEANOR ROOSEVELT

~ How Can You Apply This to Your Life Today ~

~ DAY 8 ~

NOTHING CAN SEPARATE YOU FROM HIS LOVE

EPHESIANS 3:16-19

that according to the riches of his glory he may grant you to be strengthened with power through his Spirit in your inner being, so that Christ may dwell in your hearts through faith – that you, being rooted and grounded in love, may have strength to comprehend with all the saints what is the breadth and length and height and depth, and to know the love of Christ that surpasses knowledge, that you may be filled with all the fullness of God.

No matter where you are today, no matter what you may be facing or what you have in your past, He loves you! He loves you more than anyone has ever loved you or ever will love you!

As it says in Romans 8:38-39, "For I am persuaded, that neither death, nor life, nor angels, nor principalities, nor powers, nor things present, nor things to come, Nor height, nor depth, nor any other creature, shall be able to separate us from the love of God, which is in Christ Jesus our Lord." (KJV) He loves you so much that nothing can separate you from His love, not even you!

God created each of us with this overwhelming desire to be loved! He seems to have been trying to teach me since I was a very small child, that it is only His love that can truly fill that void! Maybe the reason He has allowed me to feel an overwhelming need for love all my life was so I could tell you today that He will fill that need for you if you allow Him to. There is really no other real reason for why I felt that void even as a small child because I grew up in a loving home with godly parents, no they weren't perfect, but they loved us and told us they loved us, there was no doubt about their love for their children. But, I know what it is like to desperately want that void filled (I used to sit on the steps of the house when I was really little and hug my collie dog and cry my heart out to him saying, "nobody loves me Spike"~ and then they sold the dog, sounds silly but it went really deep in me that somehow I was lacking in a very deep way and that void in my heart was overwhelming) and I know what it is like to look for it "in all the wrong places" and I am here to say, no one on earth can fill that void like God can! God's love is meant to fill that "void" in your life and any other love is meant to be icing on the cake! He loves you so much! He knows when you hurt, He knows about every tear you have ever cried and He wants to heal your wounded heart! He wants His best for you, but you must find it in Him!

We all know that while we are in this world we will all face heart-aches and struggles, sometimes it can make you long for heaven, but He wants to help you through all of that! He wants you to have His peace and He wants you to feel His love through the storm! He wants to carry you when you just can't make it one more step! He wants to give you back your zest for life and it is found only in Him! Don't think for a moment that getting married is going to solve all your problems! You are precious in His sight and you are His bride! He loves you more than words can say! If you are married and you have never felt so alone for all that you are going through in your relationship, you can know that you are never alone; God loves you and He is right by your side. He wants to guide you in all that are facing today! He will be your rock and your strength! He will be the light that shows you the way you are to take! He will reveal the truth in His time and He will carry you through! You just need to give it all to Him today and trust Him! No one will ever love you more than He does! You can trust Him!

So, no matter what you are carrying today, you can know that the God of all creation loves you and wants you to experience love like you have never experienced and it is only found in Him! Seek Him today in all that you do! Know that He has your back and that if you will just trust Him, truly the best is yet to come!

Quote:

"What lies behind us and what lies before us are tiny matters compared to what lies within us."
RALPH WALDO EMERSON

~ How Can You Apply This To Your Life Today ~

~ DAY 9 ~

HE'S RIGHT THERE WITH YOU

ZEPHANIAH 3:17
"The Lord your God in your midst, The Mighty One, will save; He will rejoice over you with gladness, He will quiet you with His love, He will rejoice over you with singing."

If you let Him, He wants to be there for you! "The Lord your God in your midst" – remember that today, He is with you! Whatever you are facing remember that "The Mighty One will save you, He will rejoice over you with gladness, He wants to quiet you with His love and rejoice over you with singing!"

Maybe you don't feel like you deserve all of this today. Does the sin of your past seem too close to your present? The fact that you love God and you have asked for His forgiveness is enough reason for Him to want to rejoice over you with singing! He wants to quiet all of your fears and frustrations with His love! When we have a child that is rebellious there is nothing more exciting than seeing them turn around and get their lives back in order – how much more do you think your creator feels that way about you?

Are you afraid you may make the same mistakes again or maybe someone else will hurt you again or maybe you are afraid that your finances will never turn around? Whatever you are afraid of He will save you from yourself and He will give you the strength to face anything that comes your way in the future. He, The Lord Your God has chosen to be in your midst today so don't allow Satan to feed you lies that will keep you defeated and downhearted today!

I would encourage you today to rejoice in the fact that you have a God who loves you and wants to rejoice over you and be with you! Don't push Him away, draw close to Him and allow Him to love on your hurting heart. Remember Jeremiah 29:11 today; "For I know the plans I have for you, declares the Lord, plans for good and not for evil to give you a future and a hope!" The best is yet to come so don't allow Satan to rob you of that today!

Quote:

"Failure is an event, not a person. So regardless of what happens along the way, you must keep on going and doing the right thing in the right way. Then the event becomes a reality of a changed life."
ZIG ZIGLAR

~ How Can You Apply This to Your Life Today ~

~ DAY 10 ~

LET HIM CARRY IT

ISAIAH 53:5-6

But he was wounded for our transgressions, he was bruised for our iniquities: the chastisement of our peace was upon him; and with his stripes we are healed. All we like sheep have gone astray; we have turned every one to his own way; and the Lord hath laid on him the iniquity of us all. (KJV)

There is no peace outside of God and true healing comes through Him as well. Jesus death on the cross not only brought us salvation (which would be enough) but it also brought us the ability to have peace, hope, and healing in our lives. So often just as this verse says we try to go it alone and take care of our problems or carry the weight of them on our own shoulders and then we wonder why there's no peace in our lives. Jesus died on the cross to take those burdens from you so why do you want to carry it all yourself?

There's no love that can compare to Jesus love as He laid down His own life for us, not only to cover all of our sin but to bring us healing, hope, peace and a true walk with Him. With the power of God living within you through the Holy Spirit after you have been saved all these things are yours if you allow Him to fully rule in your life. Don't waste another day carrying everything yourself, He paid a dear price to carry it all for you so put it at the foot of the cross.

I have no idea what you may be facing today but please know that Jesus paid such a dear price to take all of your burdens and sin on Himself all you have to do is accept the forgiveness of sin and lay your burdens at His feet for Him to take. He loves you beyond anything you can imagine – trust Him!

Quote:

"Attitudes are nothing more than habits of thoughts, and habits can be acquired. An action repeated becomes an attitude realized."
PAUL MYER

~ How Can You Apply This to Your Life Today ~

~ DAY 11 ~

DIG DEEPER

HOSEA 10:12

Sow for yourselves righteousness; reap steadfast love; break up your fallow ground, for it is the time to seek the Lord, that he may come and rain righteousness upon you.

It is time to truly seek God! It is time to "break up your unplowed ground", in other words, look for Him in ways and places you never have before. Look for Him and seek to know Him with more drive and passion than you ever have! We miss out on so much when we settle for making Him a casual acquaintance. Ohhhh, to dig deep and know the fullness of His love, mercy and compassion for us. The more you know His love, the more you want to live for Him!

When you fall in love, you want to get to know everything there is to know about that other person. You learn what their favorite foods are, their favorite color, it is like you just can't get enough of knowing everything there is to know about him. God wants you to fall in love with Him and He wants you to have a passion to know Him better so He can shower His righteousness on your life. He is a God who is present on purpose! He isn't a God far off, He keeps track of your every tear, He knows every thought you have and He has a plan for your future, but in order to fully complete His plan for your life you need to seek Him with your whole heart.

Ask God today to give you such a desire to know Him that it becomes your greatest passion. How much would our world change if we would take the time as Christians to know Him more and live our lives in a way that reflected Him. His best will be found in seeking Him!

Quote:

"If you would lift me up you must be on higher ground."
RALPH WALDO EMERSON

~ How Can You Apply This to Your Life Today ~

~ DAY 12 ~

IS HIS LOVE SHOWING THROUGH YOU

1 JOHN 4:7-8
Beloved. let us love one another, for love is of God; and everyone who loves is born of God and knows God. He who does not love does not know God, for God is love. **(NKJV)**

So, the question of the day ladies is this: if the only thing others had to base whether or not you have a close walk with God was the love and kindness you show to others what conclusion would they come to?

Loving others isn't something we are to do when we are in the "mood", loving others is a command: 1 John 4:21 "And this commandment we have from Him: that he who loves God must love his brother also." (NKJV) God has never said, "pick and choose those people that deserve your love today, you know the ones who know your deep dark secrets and will take them to the grave, those who have enough money and right clothes, etc." God expects us to show His love to everyone so they will be drawn to Him. It is amazing how many things God says "do" in the Bible and we seem to pick and choose which ones will fit our day.

God loves us and His desire is for that love to flow through us to the world around us. If you just ask Him to speak to your heart about areas you are not doing this in trust me He will show you! We are to be obedient to God in all that He asks and this is truly the most simple command He gives us ~ love others like He loves us. How are you at a restaurant? Do you treat your server like he/she is somehow beneath you? Do they have to jump through your hoops in order to get a decent tip, let alone a 20% tip like you should be giving? Trust me I have heard those excuses of, "well if I only give God 10% why would I tip a server 20?" Hmmmmm, so you "tip" God 10%? I'm sorry that 10% is His, you didn't "give" Him anything He needed other than your obedience, but He has commanded you to love those around you and a server's wage is based on her tips because her hourly wage is only $2 and some change most of the time ~ be known for your love. Don't leave a 5% tip and then a track telling about the love of God........ How about that single Mom in the church, how could you show the love of Christ to her? What about the little children that come to your church on a bus or someone picks them up and they are a bit grungy ~ do you think maybe they could use a hug today? What about the homeless people in your area?

Ask God to show you when and where to show His love to others. Don't hold His love back from those around you, be known for it! I would encourage you to begin at home, show the love of Christ to those you live with. How much better response do you think you will get from your family if you take them off your "potters wheel", give them to God and love them where they are? Not easy but trust me you will feel better not carrying the weight of perfecting those around you and just loving them instead so God can work in their lives. I will close with this verse; 1 John 4:12b "if we love sone another, God dwelleth in us and his love is perfected in us." Ask Him to give you His love for others!

Quote:

"If you judge people you don't have time to love them."
MOTHER TERESA

~ How Can You Apply This to Your Life Today ~

~ DAY 13 ~

THERE ARE NO LIMITS

MATTHEW 7:12
"So whatever you wish that others would do to you, do also to them, for this is the law and the prophets." (ESV)

We all have to admit that how others treat us is very important to us. Are you as concerned about how you treat others? We need to be more attentive to how we treat others with our words and behaviors even if it is only for the sake of our testimony.

Ask yourself this question: if someone else treated you or talked to you the way you do them what would you think and how would it make you feel?

Jesus was a great example of showing others grace and love. Did He ever get angry or frustrated? Yes, but He didn't sin in His anger even when He threw the money changers out of the temple. Jesus showed compassion to everyone He met, He loved people and we can do the same with His help.

If you are struggling with someone in this area pray and ask God to help you love them. Ask God to fill you with His love toward them and for Him to help you respond to them in a way that they will see Him through you. 1 Corinthians chapter 13 talks about love and the fruit of truly loving others, I think most of us would struggle to meet all of those definitions but we can love better than we do today. If there is one thing so many people are missing today it is to see love. There are a lot of hurting people out there, a lot of which are children and they need someone to come alongside them and show them God's love for them.

We are not limited by age, race or finances to show the love of Christ to others, so I would encourage you today to ask Him to show you any areas you are lacking His love for someone else. Ask Him to show you how to love others better. Love will change another persons heart and life faster than all of the instruction and criticism you can muster. Allow God to love others through you today!

Quote:

"Graciousness is more than good manners. It is more than courtesy. It is the etiquette of the soul. True graciousness has such a divine quality we feel it is something that comes through us and not from us."
FRED SMITH

~ How Can You Apply This to Your Life Today ~

~ DAY 14 ~

FIND YOUR CONFIDENCE IN HIS LOVE FOR YOU

2 TIMOTHY 1:7
For God has not given us a spirit of fear,
but of power and of love and of sound mind. (NKJV)

So, what kind of life are you living today: Are you living a life full of love and feelings of empowerment and knowing that you can take on the world and win today, or are you living a life full of fear and doubt and low self-esteem, feeling as though you aren't sure how to make it through another day? Feelings of failure, self doubt, feeling as though you can never do enough to be truly loved and accepted, worthlessness all are lies of the devil, trying to defeat you and keep you from all God has planned.

God doesn't want you to live in fear! God loves you more than words can say and when someone truly loves you, they don't want you to live in fear, they want to build you up to be all God created you to be. God loves you and wants to empower you! He wants you to feel loved, appreciated and able to do all He created you to do. He wants to fill you with His peace, knowing He is there for you and He will carry you through the tough times. He wants to see you succeed and walk in His confidence of all He created you for!

So, if you are living in fear and self doubt, how exactly are you supposed to rise above all of that you ask! Well, depending on what you are living with on a daily basis will determine just how much of a battle you will have, but no matter what, you can resist the lies and overcome! If you are living with someone who is constantly tearing you down, this will take a bit more effort and determination than if it is just you tearing yourself down, but you can do it, God will see you through!

First thing to do is figure out what lies you are believing ~ you hear them all day whether they are from someone else or yourself! There are negative thoughts running through your mind, what are they? Listen and every time you hear one, write it down. At the end of the day take that list and for every negative thing you have either said to yourself or someone else has said to you about you, write down what you know deep down inside Jesus would say about you: "you are loved, you are worth dying for, you are beautiful, you are full of potential, you can accomplish all God created you to accomplish, you are worthy, you are precious, you are special, you can do whatever you set your mind to do!" When you are done ~ tear that list in half and burn the negative side and keep that positive side with you all the time so when the lies come, you can pull it out and read it again! You can do this!

As you work at becoming all you were created to be, know that Satan will fight you with everything he can, because he doesn't want to see what you may accomplish if you realize your full potential! Keep 2 Timothy 1:7 close and also keep in mind these verses as well: Ephesians 6:10-13, "Finally, my brethren, be strong in the Lord and in the power of His might. Put on the whole armor of God, that you may be able to stand against the wiles of the devil.

For we do not wrestle against flesh and blood, but against princi-palities, against powers, against the rulers of the darkness of this age, against spiritual hosts of wickedness in the heavenly places. Therefore take up the whole armor of God, that you may be able to withstand in the evil day, and having done all, to stand." (NKJV) You can stand! He will give you the strength to stand. God doesn't just want you to survive, He wants to give you the strength to thrive because that is what He created you for! Is it easy? No, that is why it is called a battle! You are fighting for yourself and those you love. Lean on Him, trust Him to give you what you need to win this – you were created to walk in His confidence, as royalty, He created you to succeed as you follow Him in all you do! The best is yet to come!

Quote:

"First we make our attitudes. Then our attitudes make us."
DENNIS WAITLEY

~ How Can You Apply This to Your Life Today ~

~ DAY 15 ~

HIS GRACE IS A SHINING EXAMPLE OF HIS LOVE FOR YOU

MATTHEW 26:75

And Peter remembered the word of Jesus who had said to him, "Before the rooster crows, you will deny Me three times." So he went out and wept bitterly. (NKJV)

Have you ever been in a situation where you knew you failed God? You should have taken a stand but for whatever reason; someone was there that you wanted to impress or that thing you wanted to spend money on was calling your name and you just couldn't say "no" so you used your tithe or maybe you knew you needed to control your mouth but you got caught up in the moment, maybe there is a guy that you just know you are not sup-posed to be sharing your heart with because you are married but you took your problems to him instead of God, whatever the case may be the guilt afterward consumed you and you felt distant from God. How could God forgive you and how long would it take to get your relationship with Him back?

Have you read this whole story about Peter? In Mark 16:7 we read where the Angel told Mary Magdalene and Mary the Mother of Jesus, "go tell his disciples and Peter that he is going before you to Galilee. There you will see him, just as he told you." Jesus knew Peter's heart and God saw the tears Peter cried over his denial of knowing Jesus. Jesus loved Peter and wanted Peter to know that he was forgiven and was still going to be used mightily by God. God didn't want Peter's mistakes to hold him back by Peter feeling defeated. It is more difficult to live right if we believe that God is always just sitting there waiting for us to do something wrong – does He discipline us? Yes, because He loves us and wants what is best for us, just like a parent who wants what is best for their children. If you love your children you discipline when needed and you don't just allow them to behave any way they choose because it is for their own good to learn right behaviors, attitudes and choices for life and when we have to discipline we still love them all the way through it and it usually breaks a parents heart to have to. God's love far exceeds anything you could have ever done, if He disciplines you it is because He loves you, but His love is always ever present and He is not far away. Here is a quote from C.H. Spurgeon:

"When I thought God was hard, I found it easy to sin; but when I found God so kind, so good, so overflowing with compassion, I smote upon my breast to think that I could ever have rebelled against One who loved me so, and sought my good. It is God's kindness that leads us to repentance."

Whether it is you that needs God's grace today or someone you know, choose to accept that God's grace and forgiveness far exceeds anything you could have done. There is a difference between sinning and choosing a lifestyle of sin. When there's no repentance in one's heart then that person cannot expect grace and forgiveness but when you pour your heart out and you are sorry for sin in your life, God's mercy abounds. Choose today to live in the freedom that repentance, salvation and a life of following

Christ will bring. Choose to live for Him today, nothing from the past matters if it is under the blood of Jesus. Let His light shine through your life so others will want Him too!

Quote:

"Failure is the opportunity to begin again,
this time more intelligently."
HENRY FORD

~ How Can You Apply This to Your Life Today ~

~ DAY 16 ~

WE ALL NEED LOVE

1 JOHN 3:18

Dear children, let us not love with words or
speech but with actions and in truth. (NIV)

The Apostle John spoke a lot about love, right down to describing himself as the disciple that Jesus loved. We all desire to be loved, it is just a built in need and some seem to have a deeper need and desire for it than others. Let's face it, if there is one type of communication that everyone in the world understands it is love!

If you aren't sure how to reach that person you work with or that lives next door, or maybe an adult child of yours that is on the wrong path, they will understand and accept your love before they will any other type of input you may have. We don't have to love someone's behavior in order to show the love of Christ! If you ask Him and allow Him to, God will fill you with His love for others.

If you are the one today that is hurting and feeling lost and alone and unloved, pour your heart out to Him and ask Him to help you see His love for you! He can and will show you, if you will just open your heart up to it! There is no greater love than His. You won't find it in the bar, or online or by desperately seeking it! One of the toughest battles we struggle with can be our desire for someone to love us, unfortunately it can cause people to make desperate decisions. Any decision you make out of desperation is probably not a good one, so be very careful!

Take some time today to show the love of God to someone else! Ask God to show you the people around you that could use a dose of His love today! Strive to be known as someone who is loving and kind, someone who truly displays the love of God. The world is a tough place full of hurting people, there can never be too much love spread around!

Quote:

"We may not be able to do any great thing, but if each of us will do something, however small it may be, a good deal will be accomplished."
D.L. MOODY

~ How Can You Apply This to Your Life Today ~

~ DAY 17 ~

HOW MUCH DO YOU LOVE HIM

DEUTERONOMY 6:5
"You shall love the Lord your God with all your heart and with all your soul and with all your might. (ESV)

Do you love Him that much? I mean so much that it almost hurts. Do you love Him with your whole heart and soul and strength?

If we would love Him that much just think of how much more we would do for Him, how much more would we be like Him and how much less we would choose to sin. If you love Him that much you certainly wouldn't choose a lifestyle of sin.

The more we know Him, the more we naturally love Him and the more we become like Him! God commanded us to love Him because He knows that the more we know and love Him the more we will stay away from those things that destroy us! (namely ~ sin) The more we love Him, the more we will love others and the more we will care about what He cares about! So, do you really love Him or is He just more of a figure that you pull out when you need something or you need His help? God's best is found in loving Him.

God loves you so much! Think back over the past and all the things He has done! Read your Bible and be reminded of all He has done for His people over the years! You are His Princess! He loves you so much and all He is asking is for your love in return! He has your back, He has your plan so throw yourself into getting to know Him better and love Him more! The best is yet to come!

Quote:

"We can do no great things ~ only small things with great love."
MOTHER TERESA

~ How Can You Apply This to Your Life Today ~

~ DAY 18 ~

NO OTHER LOVE CAN COMPARE

PSALM 59:17

O my Strength, I will sing praises to you, for you, O God, are my fortress, the God who shows me steadfast love. (ESV)

Most of us ladies grew up with the desire to one day have our prince in shining armor come along and swoop us off our feet and desperately love us and no one else for the rest of our happy lives! We love the fairy tales like Cinderella and the romance novels and the main reason for that is because there is such a deep desire for the romance and love in our lives to be fed.

The big thing we fail to realize though most of the time is that even the love of a good man will not fill that longing completely and the reason for that is because God didn't ever want us to decide we were fine without His love! Now ladies catch this though, God can and will fill that need for you completely if you allow Him to. I am not saying that you will never want a man to love you again, I am saying you will not be desperate for it.

There's no love on earth that can fill us completely like the love of God can! He loves us so completely and wholeheartedly that nothing can compare. His love doesn't change from day to day even in our weaknesses and mistakes, He loves us the same. Once we can comprehend this thought, that He is our knight in shining armor and the love of our lives then when any one else loves us it is icing on the cake! That way too when those who love us hurt us we don't fall apart and totally lose perspective on life, it hurts desperately but our Strength, our Fortress, The God who shows us steadfast love will show up and heal our wounded hearts and give us the strength to carry on in spite of the damage done by those who should love us.

I truly believe that if there is one thing God would want you to understand about Him today it is that He loves you with His whole heart and He cares more than you can imagine about the tears you have cried, the frustrations you are facing and He will be your strength through your daily struggles if you will just lean on Him! Trust Him today!

Quote:

*"There are two ways of spreading light; to be
the candle or the mirror that reflects it."*
EDITH WHARTON

~ How Can You Apply This to Your Life Today ~

~ DAY 19 ~

GET REAL IN SHOWING HIS LOVE TO OTHERS

1 CORINTHIANS 13: 1-3

If I speak in the tongues of men and of angels, but have not love I am a noisy gong or a clanging cymbal. And if I have prophetic powers, and understand all mysteries and all knowledge, and if I have all faith, so as to remove mountains, but have not love, I am nothing. If I give away all I have, and if I deliver up my body to be burned, but have not love, I gain nothing. (ESV)

How much do you love? More than anything else God wants us to be loving and godly women. We need to learn to be genuine in our love for others. There's nothing worse than knowing that someone is just acting in their kindness. No one wants a "fake" relationship with someone just for the sake of having one. These verses are pretty clear that if you are not doing these things in love then they really don't matter. This is not a "fake it till you make it program".

Ladies, we need to be real in our love for others! If that is something that seems difficult then just ask the Holy Spirit to fill you with His love for others. People are hurting all around us and sometimes they just need to see your smile, other times they may need a hug. If you know someone that is hurting, maybe you could just take them for coffee and let them just pour their heart out or maybe they would just like to sit and have meaningless conversation for a few minutes to get away from all that they are facing! If you are pressed for time, pay it forward at the drive thru by paying for the person behind you or pay for that single Mom's gas at the pump.

There are so many ways we can reach out in love to others. Look for someone today. Take the time to just do it! Do something to show the love of Christ, something to make someone feel special and loved today! The rewards of reaching out and showing the love of Christ is so incredibly rewarding. Be genuine with those around you. Allow God to love through you and see the difference it makes in your world!

Quote:

"Resolve to be tender with the young, compassionate with the aged, sympathetic with the striving, and tolerant with the weak.... because in your life you will have been all of these.
SIMPLE TRUTHS

~ How Can You Apply This to Your Life Today ~

~ DAY 20 ~

THE FULLNESS OF GOD

EPHESIANS 3:16-19
I pray that out of his glorious riches he may strengthen you with power through his Spirit in your inner being, so that Christ may dwell in your hearts through faith. And I pray that you, being rooted and established in love, may have power, together with all the Lord's holy people, to grasp how wide and long and high and deep is the love of Christ, and to know this love that surpasses knowledge ! that you may be filled to the measure of all the fullness of God. (NIV)

Have you ever reached the point in your struggle where you begin to have difficulty reminding yourself of how much God loves you? Have you ever felt as though you were just all alone in your situation and wondered if God had turned His back on you in what you were facing? If so then it is time to dig deep and hold onto your faith. Allow Him to remind you of all of His love for you because that is where you faith is found!

If Satan can get you to believe that God doesn't really love you that much (basically the same lie he used on Eve, nothing is new with him) then he has won a mighty victory! Without the deep seated belief that God loves us, cares for us and has a great plan for us where do we find any faith to carry on? If we don't fully believe that God has out best in mind every single day then how could we stir up the belief that He will deliver us and care for us. Our deep inner strength comes from knowing just how much God loves us so don't allow Satan a foothold in your faith by allowing him to lie to you about how much God loves you and cares about what you are going through today.

Allow God to strengthen you today in His love for you, hold onto these verses and look up others that are "God's love" related. Think on John 3:16, "for God so loved the world that He gave His only begotten son that whosoever believeth on Him should not perish but have everlasting life."

According to these verses if we truly want to be filled with all the fullness of God we have to know the love of Christ that surpasses all knowledge. As the love of Christ becomes more real to us the more we can be full of faith and understanding of God no matter what comes our way. If you are hurting today and you are desperately trying to hang on ask God to strengthen you in your belief in His love for you and to increase your faith. It may not feel like it but He is right there beside you wanting to help you hold on and have victory! Pray, read His promises and turn on some praise and worship music and allow His love to comfort you and fill you! The best is yet to come!

Quote:

"It's in the struggle itself that you define yourself."
PAT BUCHANAN

~ How Can You Apply This to Your Life Today ~

~ DAY 21 ~

ARE YOU FEELING DESPERATE FOR LOVE TODAY

1 JOHN 4:9

In this the love of God was made manifest among us, that God sent his only Son into the world, so that we might live through him. (ESV)

Everyone wants to be loved! We all have a deep need in our hearts that can only be filled by love! God created us with a vacuum in our hearts that can only be filled by love and if we aren't careful we can find ourselves looking for it in all the wrong places!

For some reason I have always seemed to have a vast need in my heart for love! In some ways it doesn't really make sense because I grew up in a loving home with loving parents, older siblings who loved me..... whoa wait, maybe it's the siblings. I'm just kidding about the siblings, but even they recognized early on that I seemed to have an overwhelming need to be shown love. I was my Dad's baby girl and I knew it and he loved me and taught me so much and protected me even from myself at times! As I grew older though, that over-whelming need became a problem because there were times in my life even after my divorce that I was overwhelmed with the idea that

I needed to feel as though I was worth loving! Have you ever felt that way? Even if you are married you can feel at times as though you aren't really sure if you are loved or worth loving if you aren't careful.

I have seen women so desperate for love that they are willing to be used by men in order to have a moment where they can pretend someone cares about them. That is so incredibly sad because as much as we desire the love of someone who can give us a hug, there's no love that will compare to the love of God! You are never alone if you will just seek Him. You don't have to be desperate for that longing to be loved and feel loved to be filled in your heart! Absolutely no love on earth can completely fill that void in your heart, if it could we would find ourselves in a position where we didn't feel as though we needed God. God created us because He so desired our love, so He created us with that same incredible, overwhelming desire to be loved as well and it can only be filled by Him! You can be loved by other people here on earth and I am certain you are loved by more people than you may think, but that love will not replace the love that only He can give!

God's love is not just some superficial love, pie in the sky, kind of thing that we throw out there every once in a while! We all love to say, "God loves you" and we hope that just fixes everything so we don't have to get messy with other problems and that is wrong because it gives that "superficial" feeling of God's love. God's love for you runs so deep that He isn't going to give you rest until you seek His love and all that goes along with it. He doesn't want to just love you from a distance! He wants to get up close and personal in your life! He wants to fill you with a love so deep that any other love on earth is just icing on the cake! Your need for love can be totally filled in Him! That may not sound appealing on the surface, but once you experience it you will understand ~ nothing can compare with the love of God! Nothing! He loves you, He wants you to seek Him out, He wants to be that Knight in Shining Armor that you have waited for! Digging in and having that relationship with Him does not mean that you will never have a loving relationship here on earth, it just means you will be better at a loving relationship. You will be ready for it!

Ask God today to fill you with His love and to show you in every little way possible today that He loves you and just how much He loves you! May your cup be overflowing by the end of the day today with His love for you! The best is yet to come!

Quote:

"It is one of the most beautiful compensations in life....
we can never help another without helping ourselves.
RALPH WALDO EMERSON

~ How Can You Apply This to Your Life Today ~

~ DAY 22 ~

DO YOU REALIZE THAT GOD IS ON YOUR SIDE

PSALM 56:9B
This I know, that God is for me. **(ESV)**

Did you really know that? Do you really believe it? One of the greatest lies Satan likes to use is that God is somehow against you, that He doesn't really want what is best for you and that He is holding something back from you. Stop and think for a second; why would God do that? Why wouldn't He always want what is best for His children? Don't buy Satan's lies today, trust God and know that He is for you. No matter what you are facing or what you have done, God loves you, He wants to get you on track and He truly wants His best for you.

There are times in life that God's best for you may be to grow you through tough circumstances so you can learn to trust Him and He can show Himself mighty in your life! No matter what you are facing though you can know that God is FOR you, He loves you and is working to make things right and to grow you into all you can be for Him! He will not leave you where you are, if you will trust Him to see you through to the other side!

Psalm 56:10 says, "In God whose word I praise, in the Lord, whose word I praise, in God I trust; I shall not be afraid. What can man do to me?" What are you afraid of today? There are situations that are truly fearful situations, but no matter what it is, you can know that God is for you and you can praise Him today because He loves you and will keep you safe. Pray for God's protection and look to Him for guidance. There are situations that we need to get away from and God will guide you and protect you to get you safely out. Pray for God's leading no matter what you face and He will show you the way. Romans 8:31 "What shall we then say to these things? If God be for us, who can be against us? " (KJV)

If there is something you are called to do today and you feel as though the whole world is against you in your efforts, know that God is for you! God will provide a way where there is no way and He will lead you into all you are called to do. When you truly get ahold of the fact that God is for you, nothing can hold you back from all you were created to accomplish!

Trust God today no matter where you are in life. He will keep you safe, direct your steps, give you strength and wisdom for His will for your life, He has your back because He loves you and wants His best for your life! The best is yet to come!

Quote:

*"Faith is taking the first step even when
you don't see the whole staircase."*
MARTIN LUTHER KING

~ How Can You Apply This to Your Life Today ~

~ DAY 23 ~

HOW MUCH ARE YOU LIKE HIM

ROMANS 12:9-10

Let love be genuine. Abhor what is evil; hold fast to what is good. Love one another with brotherly affection. Outdo one another in showing honor.

We are called to be like Jesus and that is exactly the example he gave us. When Paul wrote this, he didn't seem to merely be making a suggestion to how a Christ follower should behave, it is a command from God! It is time to stop being namby-pamby Christians and take a stand, but keep all of this in mind:

Let your love for others be genuine!

Hate what is evil!

Hold onto all that is good!

Love each other like brothers and sisters!

Give more honor to each other than you give yourself! Out do each other trying!

Now, you can't just take one of those things and decide, "this part works for me"! You can't just run around loving everyone and everything, never taking a stand for what is wrong! You are also not called to condemn the sinner, you are called to hate the sin and what it does to lives! Sin is evil because of the lives it destroys, that is Satan's goal you know. There are times that God may lead you to address something someone is dealing with, but make sure you are God led, not doing it out of your own pride.

How are we supposed to handle it when someone we love comes to us and tells us there is something sinful they are struggling with or maybe they have given up the struggle and are now just living there? God help us, we are to hate the sin because of what it is and what it will do in that persons life, but we are to show the love of God to that person and pray diligently for them with our whole heart, mind and soul! What if it were you? Would you be drawn in faster by people who shun you or people who are willing to express their sadness over your struggle, guarantee to pray for you and love you back into the will of God. I am not saying by any means that you act like you are ok with the sin they struggle with, I am saying you are not the judge ~ God is and He will deal with the sin, we are to pray that He draws them back to Him!

We need to keep our eyes so fixed on God that we see sin for what it is and we are so full of Him that His love just oozes out of us. Jesus didn't tell the woman who was caught in adultery that it was ok to sin, He told her to go and don't do it again! He prayed for His disciples, that they wouldn't fall into sinful behaviors, but He still loved Peter when Peter denied Him 3 times! Sin is not a gray area ~ sin is sin! Jesus had to die on the cross for all sin and that makes every bit of it evil, but He overcame sin and death, His victory is our victory and He will give anyone who asks the ability to overcome the sin in their lives. His blood covers all sin and He wants us all to have victory over all that we struggle with! Ask Him today!

Quote:

"Forgiveness is the key that unlocks the handcuffs of hate."
WILLIAM WARD

~ How Can You Apply This to Your Life Today ~

~ DAY 24 ~

CAN YOU SEE NOW THAT HE HAS BEEN PURSUING YOU

EXODUS 34:5

And the Lord descended in the cloud, and stood with him there and proclaimed the name of the Lord. (KJV)

It is amazing how the Lord pursued the Israelites and yet they were so rebellious and so willing to turn to anything that distracted them in their walk with Him through the wilderness. While God was rescuing them and trying to walk with them and have a special relationship with them they were quick to complain and go another direction.

Stop for a minute today and take a look around you; how is God pursuing you? It could be something as "little" as blessing you with a sunrise or sunset that you find unbelievably gorgeous. It could be an unexpected kindness from a friend or maybe it is something bigger like an answer to something you have been praying for. No matter where you are today in life, it's there! God is pursuing you because He so desires that closeness with you! He doesn't just bless you to bless you, He also blesses you because it gives Him so much pleasure doing it! No matter where you are in life or what you may have done, God is still pursuing you, if you are doubting that then stop for a moment and think about the fact that you are reading this, aren't you? Hmmmmm...... He loves you and He cares about you right where you are.

When you read the book of Exodus it is amazing the lengths God went to even through all of their rebellion and non stop complaining to develop that closeness with the Israelites, thus the 40 years for the 11 day journey. God was trying to get their attention so they could have the best of the best of relationships with Him. He knew if they weren't strong enough spiritually when He gave them their blessing which was the promised land, they would fall away and it would be to their detriment! He wanted what was best for them and He knew that when He first brought them out of Egypt they were not strong enough and He needed time with them in the wilderness to grow them up spiritually so they would thrive in the Promised land! He didn't just want to bless them, He wanted them to thrive once they got there!

Look for Him today and know that every little thing He does is to pursue you and to know you in the hopes you will draw closer to Him and want to know Him as well.

Quote:

"Unless you try to do something beyond what you have already mastered, you will never grow."
RONALD E. OSBORN

~ How Can You Apply This to Your Life Today ~

~ DAY 25 ~

HIS DESIRE IS TO PERSONALIZE HIS RELATIONSHIP WITH YOU

LUKE 24: 1-7

But on the first day of the week, at early dawn, they went to the tomb, taking the spices they had prepared. And they found the stone rolled away from the tomb, but when they went in they did not find the body of the Lord Jesus. While they were perplexed about this, behold, two men stood by them in dazzling apparel. And as they were frightened and bowed their faces to the ground, the men said to them, "Why do you seek the living among the dead? He is not here, but has risen. Remember how he told you, while he was still in Galilee, that the Son of Man must be delivered into the hands of sinful men and be crucified and on the third day rise." (ESV)

To me, all other stories pale in comparison to the Easter story. If you ever wonder about how much He loves you reread these verses and remember all He went through to give you freedom from the bondage of sin! It doesn't have to be Easter, obviously, for us to study this passage, I would hate to leave it out due to the dates and times of the year.

I love reading the different gospels to hear the different accounts of what happened. The stories are all the same and yet you get a little of each of their personalities mixed in so you can see how Jesus touched their individual lives. John stands out to me the most because it was obvious that He needed to feel the love of Jesus more than any of the others because he continuously talks about it. Jesus loves each of us where we are in life and He cares about what our individual needs are. We are not stamped out to all be the same and He doesn't try to reach out to us on the same levels or by the same means. We need to remember that when we see someone who doesn't quite meet our "criteria" for where they should be – Jesus loves them and so should we. That may mean we don't feel they are "spiritual enough" or on the other hand it may appear they are "too spiritual". Let God meet them where they are and show them His way, we just need to love people where they are.

Take time to really think about Jesus love for you today. Soak it up and allow Him to fill you with that love for others so they will come to know Him as well!

Quote:

"Persistence is what makes the impossible possible,
the possible likely, and the likely definite."
ROBERT HALF

~ How Can You Apply This to Your Life Today ~

~ DAY 26 ~

YOU ARE GREATLY LOVED

DANIEL 9:20-23
While I was speaking and praying, confessing my sin and the sin of my people Israel, and presenting my plea before the Lord my God for the holy hill of my God, while I was speaking in prayer, the man Gabriel, whom I had seen in the vision at the first, came to me in swift flight at the time of the evening sacrifice. He made me understand, speaking with me and saying, "O Daniel, I have now come out to give you insight and understanding. At the beginning of your pleas for mercy a word went out, and I have come to tell it to you, for you are greatly loved. Therefore consider the word and understand the vision. (ESV)

Have you been pleading with God for answers, grace, favor and or His mercy lately? Know this; God hears your prayers and He is setting about to answer you because you are greatly loved! I am by no means claiming that any of us are a Daniel but we are greatly loved and the evidence of that was all that Jesus did for us on the cross!

We should always keep a "clean slate" by confessing our sins to God and we can know with confidence that He has sent a word out to His angels to help bring His answers to pass! He cares that much! Often what we fail to take into consideration is that there are always other people involved and affected by all those things we pray for. You can trust though that your prayers aren't some big secret in heaven. He will always do what is best for you if you allow Him to, so trust Him today and know that just because you don't see your answer right now doesn't mean He hasn't already begun to put people and things in place to bring your answer to pass. God loves you and cares about all you are facing, trust Him to bring the answers you need, trust that His answer is always best!

You are greatly loved so consider the word...... Stay in the Word of God during your time of waiting! Fill your heart and mind with Him so you will be ready to receive His answer, whatever it is. Spend time day and night reading and listening to what He has to say and it will bring peace and confidence to your everyday life. I saw a church sign yesterday that said, "Feed your faith and your fears will starve." That is so true and the best way to feed your faith is to read God's word and see time and time again how God has been faithful in every way to His people and know in your heart that He will be faithful to you as well.

Quote:

"Wisdom is knowing the right path to take.... integrity is taking it."
M.H. MCKEE

~ How Can You Apply This to Your Life Today ~

~ DAY 27 ~

ARE YOU FULL TO OVERFLOWING

MATTHEW 22:37-39
And he said to him, "You shall love the Lord your God with all your heart and with all your soul and with all your mind. This is the great and first commandment. And a second is like it: You shall love your neighbor as yourself." (ESV)

How do you love? Do you love God and others with a selfless love or do you love with the idea of 'what's in it for me'? God loves us so much and Jesus was our example of total selfless love. He was willing to die for us even though we didn't deserve it. He loved in a way that drew people to Him when they saw Him.

So often in relationships, one of the biggest issues is that we love with the intent that we will get something in return. I have watched parents abandon their teenage daughters because they became pregnant instead of reaching out in love and guiding them in love because they were embarrassed. I have seen marriages where spouses don't seem to show much love unless they want something from the other or they are so needy for love, they miss truly loving anyone else.

People are hurting all around us and sometimes something as simple as a smile or a 'hello' can brighten their day. I bet there are people you are close to that could use some love without anything else attached today, no advice, no conditions, just love. There are times to just reach out in love and there are times to correct and give advice, sometimes a day of love needs to come first.

Reach out today to someone in love. Show the love of Christ to them. Allow God to fill you with His love for others and seek to bless the people He puts in your path.

Quote:

"Love doesn't make the world go round. Love is what makes the ride worthwhile."
FRANKLIN P. JONES

~ How Can You Apply This To Your Life Today ~

~ DAY 28 ~

THE GREATEST OF THESE

1 CORINTHIANS 13:13
So now faith, hope, and love abide, these three;
but the greatest of these is love. (ESV)

Don't underestimate the power of love in your situation! There are times when maybe you don't feel like extending the love of Christ to someone but you will be amazed at what God can do in that relationship whether at work, home or between friends if you do.

We cannot base whether or not we act out of love toward others on whether or not they deserve it. Too often they probably don't if we are basing it on our "human standards". We need to always remember that God loves all the time even when we don't deserve it.

How do you expect God to be able to move in your situation if you are acting out according to your flesh instead of praying for His love and attitude toward the other person and situation? People always respond quicker to love than they do anger and frustration. I get the fact that we don't always feel like "loving" but that is when we are called to pray for God's love for someone. There are no verses that say, "love your neighbor when you decide they deserve it." we are called to love regardless of what we may think or feel. Now does that mean we never take a stand or correct when someone is wrong? No. That means that we pray that God will allow His love to help us respond to wrong on every level in love. It is right to even get angry on a political level when things are done wrong but it still needs to reflect the love of Christ when we respond; in other words killing a doctor that performs an abortion is not the route to take. "Be angry and sin not!"

Quote:

"Caring about others, running the risk of feeling and leaving an impact on people, brings happiness."
RABBI HAROLD KUSHNER

~ How Can You Apply This To Your Life Today ~

~ DAY 29 ~

HAVE YOU BUILT UP WALLS

ROMANS 5:8
*but God shows his love for us in that while we
were still sinners, Christ died for us. (ESV)*

He loves you! Are you struggling with walls, where His love is concerned today because of all that life has thrown at you? Have you really opened your heart up to His pouring out His love in your life? Have you left that "honeymoon" stage of your relationship with Him? His is the only relationship that you will ever have where you don't have to lose that! You can ask for it back and He is happy to fill you with HIs love!

Life is tough and we all face struggles and heartaches, but don't mistake that for a lack of His love for you! He loves you beyond what anyone else is capable of loving you! If you have experienced the loss of your spouse, whether, by divorce or death, I would encourage you to seek the love of God before you pursue the love of another man! It isn't that there is anything wrong with another relationship if you are not married, but in order to be healthy in a new relationship and in order to be sure the love you are pursuing is right, you really will want to be full of God's love so He can direct your steps! That love void you feel is meant to be filled by Him and

Him alone so there's no love here on earth that is going to fill that void and make you feel loved and whole.

He loves you! Are you listening to Him? He loves you! He loves you where you are and just as you are and He wants to heal your wounded heart and break any chains of sin that are holding you back! He loves you and wants to make you whole! He wants to help you to become all that He created you to be! Life can be downright awful at times, so who better to walk through it with than the one who loves you and was willing to give His life for you so you can spend eternity with Him! He loves you!

Quote:

"Beautiful light is born of darkness, so the faith that springs from conflict is often the strongest and best."
R. TURNBULL

~ How Can You Apply This To Your Life Today ~

~ DAY 30 ~

REFLECTING ON JUST HOW GREAT HIS LOVE IS

PSALM 51:12

Restore to me the joy of your salvation, and uphold me with a willing spirit. (ESV)

Have you just been coasting along through life too busy to really think much about all that God has done for you? Have you gotten so caught up in all that you need to do that having a walk with God is just another "chore" of the day? Maybe you are still reading your Bible every day and going to church when the doors are open on a regular basis, but you aren't really all that excited about your relationship with God.

God wants a close relationship with you, He doesn't just want to be a picture on the wall or a book by your bed. He wants to be your best friend, He wants you to realize that He loves you and is walking with you through everything, the good times and the bad! He is that friend and companion that is always there no matter what you are facing. He loves you! Have you ever had someone in your life that you could count on when the whole world around you seemed to be messed up, you could go have a cup of coffee or glass of tea and just sit and talk and forget about all the turmoil going on? That's what God wants to have with you. You are not alone!

Have you ever been given a gift that just thinking about it still gets you excited and grateful for it? Jesus gift of salvation, the most costly of gifts, should excite us as well. It should excite us to the point that we want everyone else to experience it as well. We should have a difficult time keeping our mouths shut about it! It shouldn't be a knick-knack on a shelf.

When we have our joy that came with our salvation we are generally excited and willing to do whatever God may ask, We are ready to fight for the cause! We need to be more like that in this day and age! We need to have our joy so we will have a willing spirit to do all that God is asking us to do. We don't want to become complacent Christians without a cause. The cause is in front of us every day and I feel as though part of our biggest issue is that we are not excited about all that God has given us!

Stop for a minute today and ask God to show you if you are missing out on the joy of the salvation He has brought you. Ask Him to give you back your joy of your salvation and to give you a willing heart to serve Him, however, He may ask you to. Ask Him to help you set your priorities in a way that will make you more effective in your service for Him!

Quote:

"The measure of a truly great man is the courtesy with which he treats lesser men."
ANONYMOUS

~ How Can You Apply This To Your Life Today ~

~ DAY 31 ~

YOUR HOPE IS NOT FOUND IN YOUR FRIENDS, IT IS FOUND IN GOD

JOB 8: 3, 5-7

"Does God pervert justice? Or does the Almighty pervert the right? If you will seek God and plead with the Almighty for mercy, if you are pure and upright, surely then he will rouse himself for you and restore your rightful habitation. And though your beginning was small, your latter days will be very great." (ESV)

Job's friend was actually making a mockery of him because he was certain that Job had done something wrong for all those things to happen to him. Job was living life right and doing his best to follow God and Satan hit him on every side trying to get him to curse God. Job may have gotten frustrated with life and all that happened but he didn't curse God.

How about you? Do you feel as though you have tried to do everything right and yet things just keep getting worse with no relief in sight? Trust me I have been there and it is tough to not get frustrated with it all but the words that Bildad spoke were true in the sense that if we will just trust God and hold tight to Him and continue to do what is right God will come through and He will make your latter days better than the beginning, but that doesn't alway mean it will happen today!

Seek God today with all your heart and hold onto him knowing that He sees what you are dealing with and what you are facing and He will get you through to the other side. Remain faithful regardless of all that goes on around you and hold onto your hope in God with all that you have, don't allow Satan to rob you of it.

If you have "friends" that are not helping your situation by being negative or dragging you down it may be time to distance yourself a bit until you can see straight again. There are people who seem to think that they need to add some spiritual advice when what they should really do is just listen and encourage! Sometimes it is necessary to have a break from some people in order to be able to truly hear the heart of God and to know what He is trying to tell you about your situation. If God is removing someone from your daily communication, that doesn't mean they will be cut off forever, maybe He just wants you to focus on Him in this season! Choose godly people you can hang with and talk with that will remind you of the truth that will move you forward, and not drag you down with some "spiritual cliche". If you are that "spiritual friend, there are times it is best to just listen and allow God to do the talking! The best is yet to come!

Quote:

*"Your success or failure in life will not be decided
by the number of setbacks you encounter,
but rather how you react to them."*
SIMPLE TRUTHS *www.simpletruths.com*

~ How Can You Apply This To Your Life Today ~

~ DAY 32 ~

YOUR PRAISE
WILL BUILD YOUR HOPE

EXODUS 15:2

The Lord is my strength and my song, and He is become my salvation; He is my God, and I will prepare Him an habitation; my father's God and I will exalt him. (KJV)

When you have done all you know to do and you have poured your heart out to God and yet you still wait............ what do you do?

Praise Him!

That may sound like a way to simple of an answer for you today, but there is no better place on earth to find strength than with your hands lifted high and your heart pouring out praise to the only one who can help! I can tell you first hand that if you are lacking in faith or your heart is devastated and you can't seem to dig up any hope, praising God for who He is will fill your heart to the point of bursting with faith, hope and power for your situation! Satan would like to drag you down to the depths of despair today by getting you to believe that God doesn't care or He doesn't see or have time for you, but that is a lie straight from Hell! Absolutely nothing could be further from the truth!

Just stop for a moment and think .... Jesus............. God The Father.............. The Holy Spirit................ They love you! No one could ever love you the way they do! He created you for His glory! He wants to perform that for eternity, He wants to show Himself mighty in your life! Who is he ~ the creator of all, He is holy, He is The God of miracles, He is the healer, He is The God who is all-powerful, He has kept track of your every tear, He knows the numbers of hairs on your head (and even the number that used to be on your head), He is the almighty God, The One and Only true God who can do anything if we believe. He is the God who has promised to always do what is best and when we don't quite see eye to eye with Him on what is "best" He will always come through with the strength we need to get us through and better for it on the other side when we trust in Him!

Trust Him! Hold on to your praise! Your praise will build your hope! Turn your radio on in the car to your favorite Christian radio station or pull up Youtube and listen to praise and worship until your hope and faith is restored and you can walk in His strength! He loves you and He does have a plan! Trust Him and know that the best is yet to come!

Quote:

"Imperfect action is better than perfect inaction."
HARRY TRUMAN

~ How Can You Apply This to Your Life Today ~

~ DAY 33 ~

WHERE THERE IS HOPE FAITH ABOUNDS

ROMANS 15: 13

May the God of hope fill you with all joy and peace in believing, so that by the power of the Holy Spirit you may abound in hope. (ESV)

We all need hope and we all need joy and we need peace in believing! Where there is hope, faith abounds! Where there is no hope there is no peace or joy. God is the only one who can give you true joy and peace in believing. How are you feeling today, are you filled with joy and hope?

God wants to fill you with hope and joy and peace believing that He has it all worked out for you and His plan for your future is brighter than anything you can imagine. What seems gloomy and frustrating now will pass, we all face those crazy seasons that feel like forever and can seem overwhelming when we try to make it on our own. God never leaves you in the same season of life beyond His purpose.

Don't allow Satan to rob you of your joy and peace today! He is so full of lies and his goal is to rob you of all of the hope, joy and peace God has in store for you. He is a thief and a liar! When he comes at you with his lies, trying to remove any tidbit of hope you have left, stop him at the gates of your mind and refuse to listen. You have a choice to believe his lies or believe that the God of hope wants to bring joy and peace and more faith into your home. Hold onto Jeremiah 29:11 where it says, "for I know the plans I have for you," declares the Lord, "plans to prosper you and not to harm you, plans to give you hope and a future." (NIV) And then in 2 Timothy 1: 7 "For God has not given us a spirit of fear, but of power and of love and of a sound mind." (NKJV) God doesn't want you fearful of your future, He wants you to be confident that all that you are facing and will face He can handle, He has a plan. Nothing takes Him by surprise and He will give you the strength and resources you need to get to the other side.

Ask God today to fill you with His Joy and Peace believing so you can abound in Hope! He loves you so much and you will accomplish so much more if you are not worrying about your day. I saw a quote the other day that said, "Worry is a misuse of your imagination", I would have to say that is very well said! Hold on to the God of Hope today, reject Satan's lies and allow God's peace and joy to fill your home!

Quote:

*"Faith is knowing there is an ocean
because you have seen a brook."*
WILLIAM ARTHUR WARD

~ How Can You Apply This to Your Life Today ~

~ DAY 34 ~

HE HASN'T FORGOTTEN

JOSHUA 21:44-45
And the Lord gave them rest on every side just as he had sworn to their fathers. Not one of all their enemies had withstood them, for the Lord had given all their enemies into their hands. Not one word of all the good promises that the Lord had made to the house of Israel had failed; all came to pass. (ESV)

Did you just need some encouragement this morning that God hasn't forgotten you and all that you believe He has promised? I did! There are times that we all get to the point when we feel as though "life" has surrounded us on every side and we aren't sure which way is up any more, that is when we need to dig in and just continue to do what we know to be right.

God hasn't forgotten all that He has promised to do for us and He is still working on our behalf. Don't lose hope, hang onto your faith with all you have. Faith is dead if you are not believing anymore that God is going to do what He has said.

Psalm 43:5 "Why are you cast down, O my soul, and why are you in turmoil within me? Hope in God; for I shall again praise him, my salvation and my God." Keep your hope in God and take the time to praise Him today knowing that He will deliver you and He will keep His promises! Reach out and hold onto Him today, don't let go and expect His promises to come to pass!

These verses in Joshua came after most of the battles for the Promised land, they still had a few more enemies to face but they knew that God had already won those battles for them too before they even faced them and that is the attitude we need to have. God has won all of your battles that you are willing to give to Him. He wants to give you rest on every side but you need to continue to do right until He takes you home. We still need to keep our focus on Him and doing all that we are supposed to be doing, not on what hasn't happened yet! Even though God told the Israelites that He would go before them and He would win their battles they still had to dress for war and do their part!

Maybe this morning you are like me and you are trying to find the energy to pull yourself up and begin again. It is time; Dig deep and pull yourself up, do not focus on yourself but on the task that God is setting before you! Draw strength from Him and His promises. Look for promises in His word today that you feel you need for your situation and begin praying those promises to God and claiming them as if the reality of them are already in your life! Believe Him and go boldly before His throne to make your petitions and then you will have all the confidence you need to move ahead one day at a time. Bind Satan over your thoughts and do not allow Him to discourage you by telling you lies! Today is the first day of the rest of your life so make it a good one! God has your back and He has a plan, He isn't going to let you down now! The best is truly yet to come – keep your focus on Him!

Quote:

*"Courage does not always roar. Sometimes it is the quiet voice
at the end of the day saying, "I will try again tomorrow."*
MAC ANDERSON

~ How Can You Apply This to Your Life Today ~

~ DAY 35 ~

GOD IS THE ANSWER AND YOUR HOPE

PSALM 33:18

*Behold, the eye of the Lord is on those who fear him,
on those who hope in his steadfast love, (ESV)*

Your hope is not found in getting married, or finding a new job or in new clothes or in winning the lottery! Your hope will only be found in God! There's nothing wrong with getting married of course if God brings that right person into your life and there's nothing wrong with finding a new job or in buying new clothes when you can (Personally, I would leave the lottery alone, some people spend way too much money trying to win something that has ridiculous odds and it becomes a hinderance and addiction when they could be focused on God) God is your hope! There's just simply no other way to put it!

When you take your focus off God, you will lose your hope! Job 8:13 says, "So are the paths of all that forget God; and the hypocrite's hope shall perish." God is hope! God loves you and He cares about everything that happens in your life! He is a God of details! Nothing escapes His notice! He is the God who sees! The God who knows the future! He sees the big picture and He knows what happens right now and what job you have right now, and whether or not you are married or have children right now will affect what happens next. That doesn't mean that He doesn't want those things for you, so don't grab on to the negative here! It could very well mean that, that is His plan! His answer for you may be here! That man you are supposed to be married to may be at that new job or church, that child you are waiting for could be conceived by Christmas, you know that if you have a wayward child that it is the will of God for them to turn back to Him so you just keep pouring your heart out to God for Him to draw him/her back to Him, He wants that even more than you do! There is always hope, when you put your trust in God! Don't buy satan's lies! Don't allow what you see today discourage you because your hope is found in the God of all the Universe! Nothing is too difficult for Him! Nothing!

Please allow me to encourage you today to turn on some praise and worship music, don't turn on the sad stuff that makes you focus on the heartache and problems. Turn on some music that will boost you up and remind you of the amazing, wonderful, powerful God you serve and hold on to every ounce of hope that is found in Him! The best is yet to come!

Quote:

"God grant me the serenity to accept the things I cannot change, the courage to change the things I can, and the wisdom to know the difference."
REINHOLD NIEBUHR

~ How Can You Apply This to Your Life Today ~

~ DAY 36 ~

DON'T LOSE HOPE
AND DON'T GIVE UP

PSALM 103: 1-5
Bless the Lord, O my soul, and all that is within me, bless his holy name! Bless the Lord, O my soul, and forget not all his benefits, who forgives all your iniquity, who heals all your diseases, who redeems your life from the pit, who crowns you with steadfast love and mercy, who satisfies you with good so that your youth is renewed like the eagle's. (ESV)

Don't give up! Don't lose hope for that battle you are fighting! Bless the Lord and remember all of His benefits! He is the one who forgives your sin and will heal you! He is the one who will pull you up out of that pit you are in and will satisfy you with good again so you will feel young again! I don't know about you, but I am claiming these verses today! I need to remember all of this every day! I need to remind myself that God promises to do all of this and more in our lives so we should continuously be blessing His name and praising Him for who He is!

Satan would love to defeat you today and make you feel as though there is no hope for you and your situation, but that is a lie. God is still on His throne and He always will be so there is always hope! Unless He tells you "no" to something you are praying about, don't give up! If He does say no, know that He has a better plan. You may not understand what it is He is doing, but you can trust Him with it! Satan would like you to get so focused on your problems that you forget the God you serve is bigger than anything you can possibly face! It is all "small stuff" to the God of all the Universe! There is nothing you can face that is too difficult for God to handle! He is capable, He loves you and He is working even if you can't see it yet!

Be grateful today! Bless the Lord with all that is within you! Remind yourself of who He is and allow Him to renew your joy and hope in Him today! I love the song by Jeremy Camp, "Same Power" that reminds us that "the same power that rose Jesus from the grave ~ lives in us!" I cannot say enough that no matter what you are facing today, God can handle it! Give it to Him and trust Him! Know that He's got this! Praise Him today, bless His name because He will give you victory!

Let me clarify, because I know that things like this can get twisted; I am not saying you can just "name it and claim it" here and poof there's a Lexus in the driveway! I am saying though that we get so hung up on that kind of stuff that we don't believe God for anything! Stop being paranoid about claiming God's promises and believing Him for healing and goodness in your life! The Bible is very clear that "without faith, it is impossible to please God"! Hold on to your faith, hold on to your hope and His promises! Don't allow naysayers to get in your way today! Claim those verses that God has given you and believe Him for it! Know that beyond a shadow of a doubt, God has your best interest at heart and He sees the big picture and He knows what needs to happen in order to further His kingdom! You can trust Him with it all, regardless of His answer, but don't assume that His answer is no! Don't go this alone! He loves you and truly the best is yet to come, but you must believe Him for it!

Quote:

*"Where there is no hope in the future,
there is no power in the present."*
JOHN MAXWELL

~ How Can You Apply This to Your Life Today ~

~ DAY 37 ~

EVEN IF YOU CAN'T SEE IT, HE IS WORKING ON YOUR SITUATION

HABAKKUK 1:1-5

The burden which Habakkuk the prophet saw. O Lord, how long shall I cry, And You will not hear? Even cry out to You, "Violence!" And You will not save. Why do You show me iniquity, And cause me to see trouble? For plundering and violence are before me; There is strife, and contention arises. Therefore the law is powerless, And justice never goes forth. For the wicked surround the righteous; Therefore perverse judgment proceeds. "Look among the nations and watch ~ Be utterly astounded! For I will work a work in your days Which you would not believe, though it were told you. (NKJV)

You may not be able to see what God is working on but trust Him, He is working on your behalf! God is so good and gracious and wonderful that He doesn't always tell us what He is doing because we aren't always ready to know. He works on and in us so we are prepared for what He is about to do.

So often we are so busy praying for God to do what we want Him to do that we are blind to the work He is doing in us. Sometimes the answer doesn't lie in His "changing" that other person. Only God knows the heart and there are times that other person is just not going to change. God will put everything in our paths for us to follow Him, come back to Him when we have gone our own way, and He will do what needs to be done to draw us back to Him, but the choice is still ours. It is God's will for that person to come back to Him, but don't close the door to God working in you while you wait. Open your heart and mind to what God is trying to do in you. As He says in verse 5 above, 'if you knew what He is working on it would blow your mind.' He loves you! He wants His best for you! Allow Him to work in and through you regardless of what you can or cannot see Him doing. The change you need may be in you and it is going to be great!

Don't focus on what all you see going on around you, focus on Him. Know that you can trust Him even if it seems as though you are waiting on "nothing". Trust Him, you aren't! He is always working on our behalf, 24 hours a day, 7 days a week. There is hope! There is always hope because we serve a God who just oozes Hope and love and He wants His best for you! I would like to encourage you today to give all of your cares to Him today and allow Him to continue to work on your behalf and in you! Trust Him, knowing that when you give it all to Him and you are following Him truly the best is yet to come!

Quote:

"Persistence is what makes the impossible possible, the possible likely, and the likely definite."
ROBERT HALF

~ How Can You Apply This To Your Life Today ~

~ DAY 38 ~

HE WILL BRING YOU RELIEF

PSALM 16:8

*I have set the Lord always before me; because he is
at my right hand, I shall not be moved.* **(KJV)**

Do you feel a little shook up over everything going on around you? Are you not sure which way to turn for answers or relief? Determine today to keep your eyes on God and to remember that He is always by your side and He not only has the answers to what you are facing but He will bring your relief.

There are times in all of our lives when life can really shake us up a bit and it is in those moments that we tend to feel the most alone and frustrated. I know I have had many times when it seems as though I can barely begin to pick myself up from one thing and I get hit by something else. Who do you run to at that point? What is your reaction? Do you become full of despair and hopelessness or do you turn to God and hang on with all your might?

God wants to be at your "right side" and He wants to guide you through all that you face both good and bad. He loves you and He knows the plans He has for you. He knows what it will take to bring you into your full potential for Him and for the plans He has for your life. You don't want to settle for second best because you decide to go it alone or you decide someone else has a more tempting answer. Stick with God and allow Him to show you all that He has planned for you. Trust Him to bring it all to pass. Remain faithful no matter how bad things may seem right now. He knows, He sees what you are facing and He is right by your side to guide you if you will let Him.

Don't lose heart and don't let this world shake you up. Hold on to the steadfast hope you have in God. Trust that He truly is there to guide you and help you through – He hasn't missed a thing and He knows all that is to come! Trust Him to always do what is best! The best is yet to come!

Quote:

"It's always better to face the truth, no matter how uncomfortable, than to continue coddling a lie."
LOU HOLTZ

~ How Can You Apply This to Your Life Today ~

~ DAY 39 ~

IT'S REALLY NOT AS IMPOSSIBLE AS YOU THINK IT IS

LUKE 18:1

And he spake a parable unto them to this end, that
men ought always to pray, and not to faint; (KJV)

Have you about given up on praying about it? Don't lose hope! God will do what is best and right in your situation so hold onto your faith in Him! Luke 18:27 And he said, "The things which are impossible with men are possible with God.." (KJV) We may not always get the answer we want, but the answer is always the right answer from Him!

That situation that is seemingly impossible to you, is simple for the God who created all. Stop worrying about it and give it all to Him! We can get so caught up worrying that we lose sight of God and what He has in store for us! We all face things at times in life that are seemingly overwhelming odds and there seems to be no possible way for it to work out and then comes God with the answers. You cannot see all that He is doing and you cannot see the big picture that is why we must have complete and blind faith in Him. We have all prayed for things before and then never quite understood why

He said no when everything about it seemed good and right. God loves you and cares about every detail of your life and the lives of those you love, you must trust that His answer is always best.

Satan will always try to defeat you with his lies that God doesn't care or that God is just trying to withhold something good from you (same lie he has used since Eve) so you must hold on to your faith. Spend time in God's word and make sure you get alone with Him to pray. Pour your heart out and put your faith in His goodness, love and wisdom for your situation. Nothing is too tough for God to handle!

Quote:

"To accomplish great things we must not only act,
but also dream; not only plan, but also believe."
ANATOLE FRANCE

~ How Can You Apply This to Your Life Today ~

~ DAY 40 ~

WHEN YOU ARE GOING DOWN FOR THE LAST TIME

PSALM 120:1

In my distress I called to the Lord, and he answered me.

Are you stressed out, frustrated, tired of waiting, feeling as though you are drowning, wondering where God is and on the verge of just throwing in the towel and giving up? Maybe you are just one of those things and haven't quite gotten to all the rest. Wherever you are, God is there! He does care and He will hear your cries for help and He will deliver you!

This verse is for you today: "For I know the plans I have for you, declares the Lord, plans to prosper you and not to harm you, plans to give you hope and a future." Jeremiah 29:11 (NIV) Tell Him about it today! Tell Him how frustrated you are! Pour your heart out to Him and expect Him to answer you and deliver you!

No matter what it is you are facing, your hope will always be found in Him, so don't give up! Psalm 42:11 says, "Why are you cast down, O my soul, and why are you in turmoil within me? Hope in God; for I shall again praise him, my salvation and my God." (ESV) Know that "this too shall pass"! It didn't come to stay ~ it came to pass! This situation you are facing will not last forever as hard as that may seem to grasp right now in the heat of it all! God loves you and He will carry you through.

I know some of you face dangerous situations as well as frustrating, please let me encourage you to listen for His quiet voice and allow Him to move and guide you. As you do that, keep this verse close Psalm 91:4, "He will cover you with His pinions, and under His wings you will find refuge; His faithfulness is a shield and buckler." (ESV) He is always right there with you!

My prayer today is that whatever you may be facing, that God will show Himself mighty in your life! I am also praying that you will seek Him with your whole heart and that you will have the strength to hold on! One last verse to close with, Isaiah 40:31, "but they who wait for the Lord shall renew their strength; they shall mount up with wings like eagles; they shall run and not be weary; they shall walk and not faint." (ESV) The best is yet to come!

Quote:

"Faith believes in spite of the circumstances
and acts in spite of the consequences."
ADRIAN ROGERS

~ How Can You Apply This to Your Life Today ~

~ DAY 41 ~

HOLD ON TO THE FACT THAT GOD IS STILL ON HIS THRONE

PSALM 119:162
I rejoice at your word like one who finds great spoil. (ESV)

I desperately wanted to put an exclamation mark after that verse! Ladies, we live in a wonderful and yet terrible time. We have so many conveniences if you stop and think about it that were not known years ago and yet the world seems to have gone mad. All of the conveniences in the world don't make up for how far away from God people have gotten. I am even appalled at the anger I see when I drive anywhere. The slightest thing seems to bring out unwarranted anger. What the Bible says is wrong everyone is trying to say is right these days, there are constant threats of war everywhere you turn and acts of terror ……. the world has gone mad……… but God is still on His throne!

So, what are you to do when it seems as though your world is falling apart around you? What happens when your finances seem to have exploded and you are trying to figure out how to put the pieces back together? What can you do when you find out that your spouse is cheating on you? What do you do when your children are living a life that leaves you broken hearted for them? Where can you find hope when the loss you have experienced is overwhelming and you just can't seem find your way out from under the heavy cloak of darkness that seems to be covering you?

Psalm 120:1 says, "In my distress I cried unto the Lord and he heard me." and then in chapter 121, verse 1 and 2, "I will lift up mine eyes unto the hills, from whence cometh my help? My help cometh from the LORD, which made heaven and earth." (KJV) Wow, think about it! Your help comes from the Lord who made everything you see, and then some! Could anything you face be too difficult for Him to handle? Could He possibly carry your burdens for you and give you the strength to face another day? Could He mend that wounded heart of yours and restore it?

When you are facing fears of all of the danger surrounding you, where can you turn? Psalm 121: 3 − 8 says, "He will not let your foot be moved; he who keeps you will not slumber. Behold, he who keeps Israel will neither slumber nor sleep. The Lord is your keeper; the Lord is your shade on your right hand. The sun shall not strike you by day, nor the moon by night. The Lord will keep you from all evil; he will keep your life. The Lord will keep your going out and your coming in from this time forth and forevermore." (ESV)

What I am trying to tell you is this: No matter what it is you face today, your hope is found in Him and in His Word! That is why I wanted to put an exclamation mark at the end of the verse at the top! God's treasure for your soul that will give you hope for your day is found in His word! If you need answers, if you need hope, if you need more faith, if you need healing, the place to look is in His word! Pour your heart out to Him and ask Him to give you what you need as you read His word. Draw close to Him and allow Him to draw close to you! Don't miss out on all of the wonderful things in His word today! His word is truly like treasure! There is so much in His word that we will never fully understand or comprehend it all, but I would encourage you to dig in, even if it is one verse at a time until you find you just can't seem to get enough of it! You will find the Hope you need in there and the healing and the love you have so desperately longed for! Look for it! Ask Him to guide you! Whatever you do, don't miss out on one more day of all the treasure He has in store for you in His word! The best is yet to come!

Quote:

"Do what you can, with what you have, where you are."
THEODORE ROOSEVELT

~ How Can You Apply This to Your Life Today ~

~ DAY 42 ~

HE DIDN'T BRING YOU TO THIS POINT TO LEAVE YOU THERE

JUDGES 20:22-23

But the people, the men of Israel, took courage, and again formed the battle line in the same place where they had formed it on the first day. And the people of Israel went up and wept before the Lord until the evening. And they inquired of the Lord, "Shall we again draw near to fight against our brothers, the people of Benjamin?" And the Lord said, "Go up against them." (ESV)

The tribes of Israel had gone to the tribe of Benjamin to ask them to take care of the people who had sinned against God and the Levite who had spent the night in one of their villages. Some wicked men of the city had used and abused the Levites concubine and killed her. The Benjamites refused to "purge the evil" by giving up the men who did it so the other tribes had to fight the entire tribe. The first time they went against them, they were defeated and that is where we find them in the verses above. The verses after these state that they were defeated again so they went back to the Lord to ask again and they offered sacrifices and burnt offerings and the Lord told them to go up against them again and He would deliver them.

They were trying to do what was right, just maybe not in the right order but they were following God's leading to purge the sin from the tribes of Israel. It can be pretty tough when you know you are doing what God has told you to do and you feel as though the enemy is running you over. Do you feel that way today? Don't lose your hope! If you have followed the will of God, He is working on it and you will pull through and it will be better than it ever was before. Don't turn and run from the enemy, whatever the enemy may be in your life. Know that God will deliver it all in to your hands and He will give you victory, but you need to hold on to all that He has shown you and told you to do. There are always battles or struggles in life, don't be defeated by giving up. Keep fighting those battles until God hands you the victory He has in store for you! Don't give up!

Ask God for His direction, ask Him for His strength and then pull yourself up and go after that battle with all that you have and all that He gives you! Shake off the old and focus on what lies in front of you, don't focus on the loss, focus on the victory! Don't turn around and run back to where you came from, God's best for you is on the other side of where He is taking you! If the 'grass looks greener' somewhere else, just remind yourself of all of the nasty stuff that usually makes grass look that way! God's plan for you is best! Jeremiah 29:11 "For I know the plans I have for you", declares the Lord, "plans to prosper you and not to harm you, plans to give you hope and a future." (NIV) (Hold on to your faith and believe that God will do all that He said He would do. He didn't bring you to this point to just leave you there, He brought you to this point to move you forward in life. He loves you, pour your heart out to Him and hold on to Who you know He is as well! The best is truly yet to come!

Quote:

"You may have to fight a battle more than once to win it."
MARGARET THATCHER

~ How Can You Apply This to Your Life Today ~

~ DAY 43 ~

STOP WORRYING AND HOLD ON TO YOUR HOPE

PSALM 19:1-2
The heavens declare the glory of God, and the sky above proclaims his handiwork. Day to day pours out speech, and night to night reveals knowledge. **(ESV)**

God's glory is all around us! Just take a look around you, beyond the noise of the world and all the chaos that is happening because we live in a sin filled world and take a look at all He has created! We fret and worry about the things we need God to do in our lives and we lose hope and are anxiety ridden and yet just stop for a minute and look around. Look at the handiwork of all of God's creation, the details and the beauty reminding yourself of these verses found in *Matthew 6: 25 - 33*

> *"Therefore I say unto you, Take no thought for your life, what ye shall eat, or what ye shall drink; nor yet for your body, what ye shall put on. Is not the life more than meat, and the body than raiment? Behold the fowls of the air: for they sow not, neither do they reap, nor gather into barns;*

yet your heavenly Father feeds them. Are ye not much better than they? Which of you by taking thought can add one cubit unto his stature? And why take ye thought for raiment? Consider the lilies of the field, how they grow; they toil not, neither do they spin: And yet I say unto you, That even Solomon in all his glory was not arrayed like one of these. Wherefore, if God so clothe the grass of the field, which to day is, and tomorrow is cast into the oven, shall he not much more clothe you, O ye of little faith? Therefore take no thought saying, What shall we eat? or, What shall we drink? or, Where-withal shall we be clothed? (For after all these things do the Gentiles seek?) for your heavenly Father knoweth that ye have need of all these things. Gut seek ye first the kingdom of God, and his righteousness; and all these things shall be added unto you." (KJV)

We all need hope in order to make it through our days. You will only find your hope in Him. If you are feeling today as though you have no hope, you need to dive in and spend more time with Him. Get to know Him more! Allow Him to just pour Himself in to you and all that you do. Spend time reading His word even if you have to begin by just reading a verse or two.

If you are lacking in faith, praise Him! Sounds strange doesn't it? Praise magnifies who God is and as you do that you will find that you are filled with hope and faith, knowing that the God you serve is able! Nothing is too difficult for Him! He loves you! He is the God who sees you and loves you! He knows your situation better than you do!

This morning I took just a couple minutes and flipped through some profiles of some people on Facebook who obviously don't know the Lord and their hopelessness for their situations broke my heart! If their lack of knowing Him and their hopelessness breaks my heart what do you think it does to the heart of the God who created them? The addiction struggles, the broken hearts, the feelings of being all alone where no one cares. I grew up in a godly home so sometimes I seem to forget how much of God I take for granted. I don't know what it is like to look at any given situation and not immediately think, 'well I will just pray about it'. My grand-daughters will even stop and pray if they can't find something or something doesn't work or needs to be fixed ~ there are no limits to what we will lay hands on and pray over! We pray about any little thing that comes up. Why not? "You have not, because you ask not or because you ask with the wrong motives", (James 4) We all have times of overwhelming heartaches, sometimes experience worse heartaches than most can imagine, but no matter what we face, our hop is in Him alone! He is the only answer to all of the pain and all of the struggles. One of my favorite songs right now is Mercy Me's song, "Even If" God is good and He has a plan for your life (Jeremiah 29:11) I would like to encourage you today to put all of your hope and trust in Him, knowing that in Him the best is yet to come for your life!

Quote:

"It's in the struggle itself that you define yourself."
PAT BUCHANAN

~ How Can You Apply This to Your Life Today ~

~ DAY 44 ~

HE WANTS TO RESTORE YOUR JOY AND GIVE YOU HOPE

ISAIAH 61:3B
to give unto them beauty for ashes, the oil of joy for mourning, the garment of praise for the spirit of heaviness; that they might be called trees of righteousness, the planting of the LORD, that he might be glorified. (KJV)

Is there something today that has you feeling less than beautiful, less than capable, maybe you have lost more lately than you can bare and the grief is overwhelming. What's going on that has left you in some area of your life just feeling that you aren't enough in one way or another?

God made you beautiful in every way. He has a purpose for all that He created you to be. He wants you to be able to walk in that confidence and He wants you to allow Him to help you be all you can be for Him!

He loves you and if you are mourning someone or something today He wants to restore your joy and make you stronger for all you have faced. When they were grieving in Isaiah's day they would put ashes on their heads, God is saying here that He wants to replace your ashes with a crown of beauty if you will allow Him to. God knows your every heartache and every tear you have cried and He wants to carry you through your grief and heal your broken and wounded heart. He wants to fill you with hope for your future.

If you are grieving a relationship that has fallen apart, allow God to heal your heart and guide you through. Trust me, I have been through a divorce many years ago and for some reason that first year can be a mess if you don't allow God to love on you and guide your every move. Draw closer to Him and allow Him to bring people into your life to love on you and to minister to you in your time of need. God wants you to come out of this stronger and empowered to be the best you that you can be and He is right by your side to help make sure that happens. Change is scary and difficult at times but a lot of times change can be one of the best things that happen in your life! Allow God to guide your steps!

Hold on to your hope in Christ today and give Him all that you are facing! He loves you, knows what is best and is working right now to restore you. Stay close to Him and allow Him to bring out all the beauty you possess, all of our hope is found in Him! Truly the best is yet to come!

Quote:

"Courage does not always roar. Sometimes it is the quiet voice at the end of the day, saying, 'I will try again tomorrow.'"

~ How Can You Apply This to Your Life Today ~

~ DAY 45 ~

IF YOU MUST BE A PRISONER, BE A PRISONER OF HOPE

ZECHARIAH 9:12

Return to your stronghold, O prisoners of hope: today
I declare that I will restore to you double. (ESV)

What are you a prisoner of today? Are you a prisoner to fear, worry, negative thoughts, and addictions, what exactly are you a prisoner of?

I would like to encourage you today to give your bondage to God. I know that sounds real simple and good in words and isn't the easiest thing to do, but it is a daily choice to pick it up yourself or to give it to God. We need to choose to be prisoners of hope instead of despair and other negative things. As it says in Psalm 42:5 "Why art thou cast down, O my soul? And why art thou disquieted in me? Hope thou in God: for I shall yet praise him for the help of his countenance."

God wants to give you hope today!

When you feel discouraged and down and you are tempted to pick those things back up that are weighing you down and robbing you of your hope remember this: It is always darkest before the dawn. That is so true and you just never know how close your relief might be! Don't give up; hang on with all your might, your help is on the way!

The best comparison I can think of would be when a woman is in labor delivering her baby that she has waited so long for the biggest struggle comes just before birth! Hard labor is no picnic and I don't know of a woman on earth that can't wait until it is over but she hangs onto the fact that her "promise" is almost here so with every painful contraction she knows she is that much closer to delivery.

Satan puts on his best fight when he knows he is about to lose so of course it gets tougher when you get closer to victory in your life! Don't give up you can do this and God will pull you through!

Hold on to your hope today and pray that God will give you the strength you need – He will be there!

Quote:

"We have the right to choose our attitude."
VIKTOR FRANKL

~ How Can You Apply This to Your Life Today ~

~ DAY 46 ~

STOP LOOKING AROUND AND LOOK UP

PSALM 30:11-12

You have turned for me my mourning into dancing; you have loosed my sackcloth and clothed me with gladness, that my glory may sing your praise and not be silent. O Lord my God, I will give thanks to you forever!

There seems to be a lot of mourning going on across our nation and around the world these days. Every where you turn there seems to either be a natural disaster or there are people losing loved ones in one way or another. So many people are struggling financially and Satan seems to have come against families and marriages with a vengeance we have never seen before. Even if we look at it all and believe we are close to the end times we still need to hold onto our Hope and our Hope is in God and He can still turn our mourning into dancing!

Don't let what is going on around you rob you of your joy and your hope. Our hope doesn't come from the world running right, our hope is always from God! Whatever you are facing today don't lose hope, hold onto the faith that God will do as He has promised!

God loves you and He still has a plan for your life (Jeremiah 29:11 "For I know the plans I have for you, declares the Lord, plans to prosper you and not to harm you, plans to give you hope and a future.") nothing has changed that! Don't let the world get you down, keep pressing forward and looking to God for the answer – He's got it and He is working on your behalf if you are truly seeking His face and following Him. Do your part and trust Him for the rest!

God wants to turn your mourning into dancing today. Allow Him to cloth you with gladness so you can praise Him and be thankful forever! Let's show the world that there is a difference when your hope is in God!

Quote:

"Your success or failure in life will not be decide
by the number of setbacks you encounter,
but rather how you react to them."
MAC ANDERSON

~ How Can You Apply This to Your Life Today ~

~ DAY 47 ~

LET HIM BE YOUR HELP AND SHIELD

PSALM 115:11
You who fear the LORD, trust in the LORD:
he is their help and their shield. (ESV)

I am doing my best to make it my early morning practice to begin my day by praising God for who and all that He is, it is amazing how much it changes my perspective on life and anything I am facing when I remember first thing how mighty the God is that loves us and that we serve! To begin every prayer by praising Him for who He is not only blesses Him, it increases your faith.

What are you facing today that just seems to be a lost cause? Is it your marriage, or your finances or a child that has gone their own way? Whatever it is don't lose hope! God wants to heal your marriage, your finances and your children and whatever else you may be facing today! Marriage was not meant to be drudgery, your finances were not meant to be a mess and your children are meant to come back to the way they were raised. God is a god of all hope, a healer, a giver of all good things, He wants your children to grow up and serve Him even more than you do, he wants your marriage to be a shining example to others.

God wants to be your help and your shield today! He wants you to seek him, reverence Him for who He is and He wants you to trust Him. God is a god of power and He loves to show Himself to be the mighty god that He can be in your life if you will just have the faith to believe He will come through for you.

If you go back a few verses in this chapter verses 2 and 3 say, "why should the nations say, "where is their God?" "Our God is in the heavens; He does all that He pleases." Satan is the one who brings on the thoughts of where is God. He wants you to doubt instead of going after all that God has planned for you! God wants victory in your life because without it others will ask "where is your God?"

Ok so where can you start? Start right now by bowing your head and taking a few minutes to praise God for who He is, if you are at work don't let that be your excuse go to the closet or bathroom and take a minute and praise Him for every quality you can think of that He has! Once you have done that you will find your outlook will change, if it hasn't then go back to the closet until it does! Turn on some praise and worship music! Then take the time to ask God what you can do on your end to bring it to pass, don't take over the situation – give it all to Him and ask Him how you can help your situation. If you are married and having struggles you may need to take the first step in putting aside your hurt and frustrations and making the first move and or seek out a Christian marriage counselor. If it is your finances maybe you need to check out Dave Ramsey's program online at *www.daveramsey.com* or the money couple at *www.the moneycouple.com* If it is someone like a child or a friend that you are worried about maybe you just need to put forth more effort to pray for them and ask God to show you how you can help; sometimes you just have to get out of God's way with others and pray. Expect God to move, refuse Satan's lies and allow God to show you His faithfulness and His healing power in your situation!

My prayer for you today is taken from verses 14 and 15; (ESV)

"May the Lord give you increase, you and your children! May you be blessed by the Lord, who made heaven and earth!" Amen!

Quote:

"People were designed for accomplishment, engineered for success, and endowed with the seeds of greatness."
ZIG ZIGLAR

~ How Can You Apply This To Your Life Today ~

~ DAY 48 ~

PULL IT TOGETHER

2 CHRONICLES 15:7
But you, take courage! Do not let your hands be
weak, for your work shall be rewarded. (KJV)

As much as we all know that we need to do right regardless of our feelings or those around us there can be times when you just get weary from the constant struggle and stress going on at the same time! Some days you may feel so discouraged because no matter how much you do and no matter how hard you have sought God and the right answers you watch as others get answers or blessing as you trudge on waiting. Don't give up! "…You, take courage! Do not let your hands be weak for your work shall be rewarded."

So often the toughest challenges and frustrations come right before God's provision, blessing and rest from it all! Continue to seek God with your whole heart, don't believe the lies from Satan telling you it isn't worth it. Satan will do whatever He can to get you to give up and to go back to your own ways but that isn't the answer! It wasn't the answer before and it isn't the answer now! God's blessing and peace can only be found as you seek Him and follow Him, there's no rest found in giving up!

When you get tempted to quit and give up ask yourself this: "what am I going to gain that I wouldn't have otherwise if I quit and give up waiting on God?" Are you somehow going to "feel better" if you stop doing what you know you are supposed to do? Is there going to be rest and blessing if you quit? Probably not so why would you even go there? Hold on to the Hope found only in God! Hold onto His promises that He has a plan for you for good and not evil a plan to give you a hope and a future!

Take one day at a time. Look at today as though this could be the last day you will have to put up with this or wait! Tomorrow when you get up seek God again and face your day if it starts out the same believing that "today could very well be the day". Honor God with your words and your faith in Him! Trust Him to bring it all to pass and rejoice that the day is soon coming! Remain faithful and hold onto your hope in Him, trust Him for the strength to see you through!

Quote:

"Throw your heart over the fence and the rest will follow"
NORMAN VINCENT PEALE

~ How Can You Apply This To Your Life Today ~

~ DAY 49 ~

FINDING HOPE

PSALM 119:114

You are my hiding place and my shield; I hope in your word.

Are you just so tired of it all already that you just want to find somewhere to hide? Have you had those days where you just want to throw in the towel and quit because the battle is too much? Trust me I have had my share of those days over the years.

I remember when my children were little (toddlers) having a couple days where I literally locked myself in the bathroom for a couple minutes to pull it together. I just needed a place to hide for a minute. There are times when life does that to me now as well; I need that proverbial bathroom to lock myself in to pull it all together. Well, here's the deal; God wants to be that "hiding place" for you! When it feels as though it's all falling apart or it is just becoming too much He wants to be your place to run to. He wants to be your protection (shield).

God loves you so much and He knows how much you can take, the problems begin when you don't run to Him. Sometimes we complain because we feel as though we have just had more than we can bare but what we refuse to acknowledge is that we haven't run to Him or given it to Him we have tried to either do it all ourselves or we have looked somewhere else for the answers and then we wonder why He has allowed more than we can handle in our lives. He's been there all the time, He has asked to be your protection and your hiding place and has told you that you will find hope in His word.

If you are feeling overwhelmed today I would encourage you to ask yourself if you have done what you can and then if you have, make sure you have given it all to God. Allow Him to work out the details that are overwhelming you. Don't carry all of that on your shoulders, God wants to help. If there's something you need to do He will show you but other than that pray and ask Him what you need to give to Him.

Spend time in The Word. Look for His promises and answers to your situation. If you pray that God will give you verses for your situation He will. Don't give up if it takes you a few days to get your answers, He has a reason for His timing. Spend time alone with Him, listening and waiting, knowing that He loves you and He has a plan and it isn't to overwhelm you and frustrate you it is for your good. The best is yet to come!

Quote:

*"If you don't think every day is a good day,
just try missing one."*
CAVETT ROBERT

~ How Can You Apply This To Your Life Today ~

~ DAY 50 ~

EVEN IF HE SEEMS SILENT, PRAY

PSALM 20:1
May the Lord answer you in the day of trouble!
May the name of the God of Jacob protect you! (ESV)

What is going on when God seems silent? Do you ever have those days where you feel like you are praying and you know He is there but there seems to only be silence when you call on Him? You ask for answers and signs and yet the silence is deadening to the point where you feel as though maybe He is busy working on something else and if you aren't careful Satan will try to sneak in during those times to make you feel as though you aren't important to God and that God doesn't care.

When you are waiting on God guard your thoughts and stand firm knowing that He is still working on your behalf and the answer is on it's way. Sometimes our lessons we need to learn are in the "wait". In other words we grow in trust when we are waiting and not allowing ourselves to move into panic mode, taking our problems on by ourselves and allowing the lies of Satan to cloud our understanding that God always has our best interest in mind and He is always in control as long as we allow Him to work in our lives!

Don't get anxious, take one day at a time and allow God to move on your behalf and allow Him to grow you spiritually during the process.

This is my prayer for you today and I would encourage all who read this to pray that others who read it will have the same blessing on their lives:

"May the Lord answer you in the day of trouble! May the name of the God of Jacob protect you! May he send you help from the sanctuary and give you support from Zion! May he remember all your offerings and regard with favor your burnt sacrifices! May he grant you your heart's desire and fulfill all your plans! May we shout for joy over your salvation and in the name of our God set up our banners! May the Lord fulfill all your petitions! Now I know that the Lord saves his anointed; he will answer him from his holy heaven with the saving might of his right hand. Some trust in chariots and some in horses, but we trust in the name of the Lord our God. They collapse and fall, but we rise and stand upright. O Lord save the king! May he answer us when we call." Psalm 20 Amen!

Quote:

"Optimism is the faith that leads to achievement.
Nothing can be done without hope and confidence."
HELEN KELLER

~ How Can You Apply This To Your Life Today ~

~ DAY 51 ~

IT IS A SPIRITUAL BATTLE

1 PETER 5: 8-9

Be sober-minded; be watchful. Your adversary the devil prowls around like a roaring lion, seeking someone to devour. Resist him, firm in your faith, knowing that the same kinds of suffering are being experienced by your brotherhood throughout the world. (ESV)

No matter where you live in the world, we all face the same spiritual battle. Satan is looking for the right time and weak moment in your life to attack. He is patient and he will lurk, waiting as long as he needs to in order to catch you off guard. When we were in Africa and were out on the Masai Mara, it was amazing how easily a lion could hide in the brush, waiting for his prey to walk by! The camouflage of his fur in the brush kept him hidden and if you didn't know what you were looking for you could miss him completely! I can't really say that I would ever want to walk anywhere out there because I would be a wreck after a few minutes trying to keep all of my senses alert and eyes peeled looking for animals that could kill me! We need our senses guarded in this spiritual battle as well, but the great thing is ~ God is on your side, the battle is the Lord's and if you wrap yourself up in His armor, you are as safe as we were in the jeep, just a few yards away from those lions!

Crazy thing is; did you realize that sometimes your weakest moments come during or right after that Mountaintop experience! If you aren't careful to keep your guard up (Ephesians 6:10-18) when you have that great moment and feeling of success, you can find he has snuck in and is setting up house to destroy all God is accomplishing through you! Sometimes his attacks come from well meaning people. Sometimes they come from pride, sometimes it comes from such a fear of being pride filled, instead of relying on God to keep you humble you allow others to tell you how you need to do your ministry and you find yourself following them instead of continuing in God's leading! If there is one thing Satan is good at, it is the subtle lie! If he can get you to believe that these "godly people" know best what you should do vs. following your gut with what God has always led you to do, then he has a foot in the door! Don't misunderstand I am all for godly counsel, the Bible is clear that we are to seek godly counsel, but there are times when others want to impose their "godly counsel" and it doesn't line up with what God gave you and that is when you need to hold your ground and follow God and tell others to step aside.

Satan loves to make you think that everything is hopeless in your situation! With God, nothing is ever hopeless unless God has told you "no!". If God hasn't told you no, then you need to hold on to your faith and hope in Him! Believe that He loves you and cares about all you face and He is your deliverer ~ not just that woman down the streets deliverer, He is yours! God always wants His best for you! He wants you to have a healthy marriage, He hates abuse, He loves your children even more than you do and wants what is best for them as well so continue to pour your heart out to Him to urge Him to fight for them! God loves you! He wants you to trust Him and put all your faith and hope in Him!

This war waged against us spiritually is real and must be taken seriously! Satan wants to keep you from being all you can be for God, no matter who you are, no matter what you have, no matter where you live ~ he is after you! Great news is that God is for you and "if God is for you who can succeed against you," if you believe! (Romans 8:31) You can have victory! You can do great things with Christ! You can have deliverance from your situation! Hold on to your hope in Him! Arm yourself with God's armor! Pray!!(Hebrews 4:16 tells us, "Let us then with confidence draw near to the throne of grace, that we may receive mercy and find grace to help in time of need" ESV) Whatever you do; don't give up the fight because the best is yet to come!

Quote:

"Adversity is the first path to truth."
GEORGE GORDON BYRON

~ How Can You Apply This To Your Life Today ~

~ DAY 52 ~

HE WANTS YOU TO OVERFLOW WITH HOPE

ROMANS 15: 12-13

And again Isaiah says, "The root of Jesse will come, even he who arises to rule the Gentiles; in him will the Gentiles hope." May the God of hope fill you with all joy and peace in believing, so that by the power of the Holy Spirit you may abound in hope. (ESV)

Do you need a little hope today? Well, God wants you to abound in hope! He wants to fill you with joy and believing so you can be overflowing with His Hope!

I want to abound in Hope! How about you? Wouldn't you like to just be so filled with God's hope today that you are just vibrating with excitement for who He is and all He is going to do in your life!

No matter what you are facing today or how things look, God can fill you with His hope! He wants to fill you with His hope! One of the greatest testimonies we can have as believers is hope! The world is starving for peace, joy and hope! No one wants to follow a 'sad sack'! I may not have been where you are today, but I have seen a lot; I was raised by great godly parents, but that didn't protect me from being molested as a child and they didn't know, I was married to a man "Dr. Jeckle and Mr. Hyde who went to Bible school and yet cheated on me with several women, I was a single Mom for 14 years, I know what it is like to struggle beyond struggle financially, I was so ill a few years back I didn't think I was going to live and I am hear to tell you today there is hope! I am sure I could probably fill a few books with 'stuff' I have seen in my lifetime, but seriously the most important truth I can impart to you today is that no matter what ~ there is alway hope and it only comes from God! Our hope, peace and joy will never come from our circumstances because circumstances are always changing, but the God of hope will fill you if you will seek Him and allow Him to!

God's will is to draw you closer to Him! He wants to hold you and heal that wounded heart of yours! He wants to shower down His love, blessings and peace on your life! Give it all to Him today! Rest in His unchanging grace and allow Him to fill you with hope for what lies ahead! The best is truly yet to come!

Quote:

"You become what you think about."
EARL NIGHTINGALE

~ How Can You Apply This To Your Life Today ~

~ DAY 53 ~

HE WANTS TO GIVE YOU STRENGTH AND CONFIDENCE

ISAIAH 35: 3-4
Strengthen the weak hands, and make firm the feeble knees.
Say to those who have an anxious heart, "Be strong; fear
not! Behold, your God will come with vengeance, with the
recompense of God. he will come and save you." (ESV)

We all have the desire to be able to look forward to our futures with hope and the anticipation of things getting better! Whether it is the New Year, or a new job or a new move, or maybe a new relationship, no matter what it is we press forward with the hope that it will be better! Maybe you have been through so much lately that, that is all you have to cling to ~ 'it has to get better from here!'

Well, know this as you push forward; God doesn't want your heart to be anxious, He wants to give you the strength and confidence you need for tomorrow, knowing that He will come through for you and He will save you. God loves you and He wants you to be able to be all He created you to be. He isn't going to leave you out here on your own! He still has a plan! Don't look to be rescued somewhere else. Don't look for your answers in something or someone other than Him. Focus on God and allow Him to bring it all together!

Don't let the past discourage you! Isaiah 43:16, 18-19 says, Thus says the Lord, who makes a way in the sea, a path in the mighty waters, "Remember not the former things, nor consider the things of old. Behold, I am doing a new thing; now it springs forth, do you not perceive it? I will make a way in the wilderness and rivers in the desert." (ESV) Leave the past in the past, and trust that He will make a path where there isn't one and He will give you the strength to follow Him and to accomplish all you are called to accomplish! Today is a new day, a new beginning, a fresh start! Grab hold of His promises today and trust Him with your whole heart that He will come through! The best is yet to come!

Quote:

"Prayer reminds me, that I'm not lost in a
dream. I'm only dreaming I am lost."
NOAH BENSHEA "JACOB THE BAKER"

~ How Can You Apply This To Your Life Today ~

~ DAY 54 ~

HE DELIGHTS IN YOU AND WILL FILL YOU WITH HOPE

PSALM 18:19

He brought me out into a broad place;
he rescued me, because he delighted in me. (ESV)

God does delight in you! Not just everyone around you, but you! God delights in you and He wants to rescue you from all that you are struggling with! God often allows struggles in our lives to grow us into all we can be so sometimes the answer isn't to pull you out of what you are going through but to carry you through it!

No matter what you are facing, God is there! God is with us when we are on the "mountain tops" of life and He is with us in the valleys! The question for you is; will you allow Him to guide you through to the other side.

God wants to bring you into that "broad place" in life. A place where you have no walls holding you back, a place where you don't have to hide. He wants to bring you to a place in life where you can be all He created you to be, that path isn't always easy but it is worth it!

If you need rescuing today, don't lose hope! Hold on to your faith in God and trust Him to bring you through! God loves you and cares about every single detail of your life! God created you for this moment and for this time, sometimes other people or addictions and struggles get in our way, but His plan will still prevail if you trust Him! Write these verses down and carry them with you today:

Jeremiah 29:11, "For I know the plans I have for you", declares the Lord, "plans for good and not for evil, to give you a future and a hope!"

Isaiah 40:31, "But they that wait upon the LORD shall renew their strength; they shall mount up with wings as eagles; they shall run, and not be weary, and they shall walk, and not faint."

This thing you are facing today, may be overwhelming, but trust Him to see you through! Things don't always turn out the way we plan, but you can know that no matter what He is by your side! He loves you! He cares! He won't let you down if you will just fully trust in Him to see you through whatever may happen and whatever you may face! Give it all to Him and trust that truly the best is yet to come!

Quote:

*"Faith is taking the first step even when
you don't see the whole staircase."*
MARTIN LUTHER KING

~ How Can You Apply This To Your Life Today ~

~ DAY 55 ~

DO YOU REALLY MATTER

PSALM 119:18

Open my eyes, that I may behold wondrous things out of your law. (ESV)

Do you ever feel as though you don't matter in the Big scheme of things? Do you feel as though no matter how much you pray you just can't seem to get an answer? Have you ever thought that no matter how you follow God and no matter how much you do right you can't seem to get to the point where you feel as though it makes a difference? Maybe you feel as though what you are going through in the process of following God, all the hurt, pain, frustrations, and lack don't really have a grip on God's heart.

It's time to ask God to open your eyes to see all the wondrous things He is doing on your behalf. Ask Him to give you a glimpse today of how much He cares about what you are experiencing today and all you have felt along the way. We all know the right words to say to each other, "God loves you, He cares about what you are facing, He keeps track of your every tear," but it is ok if today you need Him to show you. It is okay if you need to ask Him to open your eyes to His love and to show you how much He cares – it's okay if you are tired of hearing it and you need to see and feel something directly from God today! Don't give up if you don't see it immediately, keep asking and looking for it, He will show you!

We know God cares, we know that He has a plan for us, I think Jeremiah 29:11 has become my life verse, I seem to quote it all the time. The reason for that is because I know how hard it can be, I get that there are days when you just feel as though maybe you are standing alone and you are hurting and wondering "why". It is okay to feel that way but don't allow yourself to live there, focus on the bigger picture and the fact that no matter what you may feel today Jeremiah 29:11 is real and true! God is working on your behalf even if it doesn't seem like it to you right now. He cares and He will bring it all together if you can just hold on to Him and His word.

Whatever it is that you may be struggling with today whether it is big or small I would encourage you to ask God to open your eyes to what He has to say about it all and to give you a glimpse of what He is doing to encourage you today. The best is yet to come!

Quote:

"*Real optimism is aware of problems but recognizes solutions; knows about difficulties but believes they can be overcome; sees the negative, but accentuates the positives; is exposed to the worst but expects the best; has reason to complain, but chooses to smile.*"
WILLIAM ARTHUR WARD

~ How Can You Apply This To Your Life Today ~

~ DAY 56 ~

HOPE IN GOD

PSALM 43:5

Why are you cast down, O my soul, and why are you in turmoil within me? Hope in God; for I shall again praise him, my salvation and my God. (ESV)

Hold onto your hope in God, don't give up now – He is still by your side! I was asking God this morning if this was really what I was supposed to be writing on this morning, I know some people get tired of hearing this sort of message but God reassured me that He has too many people out there that are hurting today and He is determined to get through to them that He loves them and He cares and He is working on it. He loves you like a Daddy loves His little girl and He is wanting to walk with you and hold your hand all the way to the other side.

I remember as a little girl we used to love to go to the Upper Peninsula of Michigan to see the incredible color of the leaves on the trees every Fall, it was just so beautiful and the color was extraordinary! There was a bridge that ran over a small valley full of trees loaded with orange, red and yellow leaves, it was breath-taking and I was overwhelmingly afraid of heights. My brother was not afraid and often had to be told to be careful but I could barely handle peering over from a distance. As soon as my Dad would pick me up though I could be at the very edge of the bridge looking over and I felt as safe as could be! That is exactly how God wants you to feel today! He's got you! He isn't going to let go, He's got you! He loves you and He wants you to see the beauty of what He has in store for you but you have to trust Him!

Hold onto your faith this morning and allow God to work in you and in your situation knowing that – He's got you! He isn't going to let you fall or allow this situation to devour you – He has better things ahead for you and He wants you to be able to rejoice in that fact because He is your God and your salvation! There are better days ahead, hold on!

Quote:

"A happy person is not a person in a certain
set of circumstances, but rather a person
with a certain set of attitudes."
HUGH DOWNS

~ How Can You Apply This To Your Life Today ~

~ DAY 57 ~

DON'T LET GO OF YOUR HOPE! HE WILL SHOW UP!

PSALM 5:11

But let all who take refuge in you rejoice; let them ever sing for joy, and spread your protection over them, that those who love your name may exult in you. (ESV)

This verse is my prayer for each of you today!

Everywhere you turn there seems to be more news of more turmoil on the earth! If it isn't weather related or fires burning out of control, or earthquakes, it is people who go crazy and kill masses of other people! Even in our every day lives, it seems that infidelity in marriage, financial issues and struggles and even addictions (often brought on by not being able to handle the every day stresses thrown at them) are all out of control. Where can we find hope, peace or joy in the midst of all of it? How do we keep from not "losing it" ourselves?

The stronger the storm rages around you the more focused you have to become! You must set your eyes on Him or you will lose the ability to do what you need to do. Is that an easy task? Absolutely not! I am hear to say, first hand, that it is very difficult when your heart is being wrenched out of your chest and/or your finances seem to be about as challenging to get under control as one of those games where you stand in a small inclosed area and money blows all around and you are supposed to catch as much as you can, or your children are rebelling or the grief you are facing is totally consuming you, or maybe you feel as though you will never get control over that addiction! I get it! But, the more it hurts, the more difficult it is ~ the more you need to focus on Him and Him alone! He will show up! He will heal! He will guide you and give you strength! He can give you your hope and joy back!

Rejoice today in the fact that He will help you and heal you! Take refuge in Him today! Take your eyes off the storm! Truly the best is yet to come!

Quote:

"Our greatest danger in life is in permitting the
urgent things to crowd out the important."
CHARLES E. HUMMEL

~ How Can You Apply This To Your Life Today ~

~ DAY 58 ~

ARE YOU DISTRAUGHT AND OVERWHELMED? THERE IS HOPE!

PSALM 38:9-10

O Lord, all my longing is before you; my sighing is not hidden from you. My heart throbs; my strength fails me, and the light of my eyes ~ it also has gone from me. (ESV)

David was obviously distraught and overwhelmed at this point in his life and yet he knew that God was watching and would deliver him. Have you ever felt this way or do you know of someone who does today? David was at the point where even the joy that shone in his eyes in previous days was gone!

God loves you beyond measure and he will strengthen you, heal your heart and give you back your joy. If it isn't you that is suffering right now maybe there is someone you know could use your ability to show them the love of Christ today. God is ever present and cares about every heartache and trial we face

.

From the way this Psalm starts and the title, it looks as though it could have been written after he had sinned and he was depressed over his consequences and the fact that he felt as though his friends had left and his enemies were going to kick him while he was down. I am sure when what he had done with Bathsheba was revealed he was miserable, ashamed and expected everyone to be against him. Our view of life can get distorted a bit when we are down if we do not keep our eyes on God. We can even get to the point where we feel that everyone is against us when really they may be just trying to stay out of our way or they aren't quite sure what to say or do.

If you are in a position to help someone else who is down ask God for direction and keep the idea in mind that they may not seem receptive but do your best to be there once they are. Don't allow yourself to be dragged down into their despair but pray for them and ask God to show them His way of escape.

If it is you who is down today ask God to guide you and to allow you to feel and see His love even in others who may actually be trying to help. Trust Him to deliver and heal you today, He cares and He hasn't missed a tear you have shed over your situation.

Quote:

"Remember happiness doesn't depend on who you are or what you have; it depends solely upon what you think."
DALE CARNEGIE

~ How Can You Apply This To Your Life Today ~

~ DAY 59 ~

IT IS ALWAYS DARKEST BEFORE THE DAWN

1 KINGS 1:38-40

So Zadok the priest, and Nathan the prophet, and Benaiah the son of Johoiada, and the Cherethites and the Pelethites went down and had Solomon ride on King David's mule and brought him to Gihon. There Zadok the priest took the horn of oil from the tent and anointed Solomon. They they blew the trumpet, and all the people said, "Long live King Solomon!" And all the people went up after him, playing on pipes, and rejoicing with great joy, so that t the earth was split by their noise.

Just moments before this Solomon and his Mom, Bathsheba, were in danger of being killed by David's other son Adonijah because he had assumed the throne without David knowing. I am sure things looked pretty dark to Bathsheba as she went to see the king, knowing that David was so old and ill that his strength was failing him and if he didn't do something quickly they would be dead.

This is not the only time in the Bible we read of someone whose circumstances were seemingly beyond hopeless; take a look at

Esther when all of the Jews were in danger of being killed including her! Take a look at Joseph when he was in prison for things he never did and one day the Pharaoh sent for him and made him ruler over the land second only to him! What about Mary, Jesus' Mom, one day she is just an every day girl engaged to be married and the next thing she knew she was going to be the Mother of the Son of God!

God still sits on the throne and no matter how dismal and dark your situation seems right now it can all be changed in a moment! God never stops working in our lives and working out His will for us as we follow Him so don't lose heart if things seem so dark around you that you just can't seem to see even a flicker of light at the end of your tunnel. God is there and He will deliver you! He will bring it all to pass!

Don't lose heart today! God is with you and He will come through, the best is yet to come! Trust Him to do what He has said!

Quote:

*"To accomplish great things we must not only act,
but also dream; not only plan, bur also believe."*
ANATOLE FRANCE

~ How Can You Apply This To Your Life Today ~

~ DAY 60 ~

ARE YOU SICK AND TIRED OF WAITING

MICAH 7:7

But as for me, I will look to the Lord; I will wait for the
God of my salvation; my God will hear me. (ESV)

Do you ever get to that point where you are just sick and tired of waiting and you are tempted to just take care of the situation yourself? Don't! Don't allow Satan to talk you into stepping in, instead of waiting on God! Trust me, I have done that enough times to know it just really messes things up, it isn't worth it! If you read the rest of this chapter in Micah you can see that God will come, He will vindicate, He will deliver you and heal you! He hasn't forgotten! Your answer could be here today!

Don't get impatient, don't lose your hope! God is by your side and His plan is in the works, even if you don't see things changing, they always are and if you will just trust Him, He will bring to pass all He has promised. "For I know the plans I have for you," declares the Lord, "plans for good and not for evil. Plans to give you a future and a hope!" Jeremiah 29:11. He hasn't forgotten you! There is hope! There is always hope and it is found in Him, not in your 'handling this yourself'! Pour yourself into His word today. Turn on the radio and listen to some positive music. Put all of your faith and trust in Him today, no matter what lies Satan is trying to get you to believe. You are more than a conqueror in Him and truly the best is yet to come and it is found in waiting on Him

Quote:

"You seldom come across anything more enjoyable than a happy person."
FRANK A. CLARK

~ How Can You Apply This To Your Life Today ~

~ DAY 61 ~

DON'T LET YOUR SELF-TALK DESTROY YOUR FAITH

HEBREWS 11:1-2
*Now faith is the substance of things hoped
for, the evidence of things not seen. For by it
the elders obtained a good report. (KJV)*

We could all use a little more faith I am sure, because we all struggle with the non-stop battle against all of the lies satan throws at us to discourage us. I don't care who you are, satan will do his best to try to discourage you in all that you do and he will throw every lie imaginable at you to make you think that God doesn't care. Since we know all of that, then that is where we need to begin!

You must begin with guarding the doors of your heart and mind. Check every thought and comment that comes in to see if it is destructive. If you are living with someone who is verbally abusive, I would seriously suggest seeking out some godly counsel to help you. If for some reason that is not available to you, believe me I have been in that situation, you can still fight it and win with God's help! Your self talk is the first thing you must check. Nothing good comes from running yourself in the ground! God made you and

He made you with potential, there are no limitations with God. No matter where you are or what you have done or anyone else has ever said about you, God wants to make you whole and He wants to build you up to be all He created you to be! Start by making a list of all of the lies you are believing about yourself or about your situation and then take that list to God and ask Him to help you write down His truth about each of those things! Remember; 2 Timothy 1:7 "For God hath not given us the spirit of fear; but of power, and of love and of a sound mind!" (KJV)

Whatever area it is in your life that you are lacking faith in, ask God for more faith! Be like the man in Mark 9:24,Immediately the father of the child cried out and said, "I believe; help my unbelief!" God wants you to have faith, He doesn't want you to be discouraged! What purpose would it serve to have a bunch of powerless Christians walking around? He wants you to believe! He wants you to be victorious! He wants to show Himself mighty in your life! He loves you and created you with all of the ability you need to accomplish all that He created you to accomplish. Trust Him! Create a list of affirmations of God's truth for your situation today and keep it with you so you can go over them any time, especially when your faith starts to waiver! Know that there is nothing that is too difficult for God and know that He wants His best for you!

Let's all commit to praying that God will move in each person's heart that reads this today to give them all the faith they need for their situation and to glorify Him!

Quote:

*"Faith believes in spite of the circumstances
and acts in spite of the consequences."*
ADRIAN ROGERS

~ How Can You Apply This To Your Life Today ~

~ DAY 62 ~

WHY DO WE LACK FAITH

MATTHEW 9:28-29
When he entered the house, the blind men came to him, and Jesus said to them, "Do you believe that I am able to do tis?" They said to him, "Yes, Lord." Then he touched their eyes, saying, "According to your faith be it done to you." (ESV)

Where would those words leave you, "according to your faith be it done to you."? I am afraid there are many times in my life that would leave me right where I was. Why do we lack in the area of faith? Why do we so often jump to believe satan's lies instead of the goodness of God and His word? We have a choice whether or not to buy into all of the negative or not, so why do we? God's word is truth!

James 4:2-3, "You desire and do not have, so you murder. You covet and cannot obtain, so you fight and quarrel. You do not have, because you do not ask. You ask and do not receive, because you ask wrongly, to spend it on your passions." (ESV) It may begin with the fact that while we are young in our salvation and not mature, we ask for all the wrong reasons or we don't ask at all and then get upset when we don't have what we need. When we ask purely for selfish reasons, not considering others or God's plan and we don't receive something from Him, we tend to blame Him instead

THE GREATEST OF THESE | 223

of seeking Him more to know what His desires for us would be. God knows what is best and it is His best that we need to ask for and seek, then we can ask with the confidence that He will hear and answer our prayers.

James 1:5-7, "If any of you lacks wisdom, let him ask God, who gives generously to all without reproach, and it will be given him. But let him ask in faith, with no doubting, for the one who doubts is like a wave of the sea that is driven and tossed by the wind. For that person must not suppose that he will receive anything from the Lord;" If you don't know what to ask for in your situation, ask for God's wisdom to know and for Him to guide you and then believe that He will and He will do as He has promised.

God loves you and He wants to give you His peace and His wisdom for your life! He wants His best for you, but you must realize that it begins and ends with Him! You must seek Him first. God is not like a fast food restaurant where you can just pull up to the little box and put your order in, He desires a relationship with you. Seek His face, strive for a closer relationship with Him by spending more time in His word and getting to know Him better! He wants to be your knight in shining armor and He wants to fill you with His love which is by far better than any love you will find on earth! He is the only one who can truly fill that void in your life and make you feel whole again. He will heal your wounded heart and will fill it to overflowing with His love if you allow Him to and you seek Him with your whole heart! Ask Him today to give you the faith you need for your situation. Be like the man in Mark 9:24, And straightway the father of the child cried out, and said with tears, "Lord, I believe; help thou mine unbelief." When you are lacking the faith you need, ask Him to help you to believe! He wants to help increase your faith!

Quote:

"Optimism is the faith that leads to achievement.
Nothing can be done without hope and confidence."
HELEN KELLER

~ How Can You Apply This To Your Life Today ~

~ DAY 63 ~

FAITH MAKES THE DIFFERENCE

JAMES 5:13-17

Is anyone among you suffering? Let him pray. Is anyone cheerful? Let him sing praise. Is anyone among you sick? Let him call for the elders of the church, and let them pray over him, anointing him with oil in the name of the Lord. And the prayer of faith will save the one who is sick, and the Lord will raise him up. And if he has committee sins, he will be forgiven. Therefore, confess your sins to one another and pray for one another, that you may be healed. The prayer of a righteous person has great power as it is working. Elijah was a man with a nature like ours, and he prayed fervently that it might not rain, and for three years and six months it did not rain on the earth. (ESV)

Prayer is so important, but it is our faith that makes the difference! It isn't the long, repetitious prayer that moves God to action, it is faith! (Matthew 6:7, But when ye pray, use not vain repetitions, as the heathen do: for they think that they shall be heard for their much speaking.) It is not perfection that will get answers for you, although if you are choosing to live in sin and you are unwilling to deal with it or ask for forgiveness and change then obviously there is a wall between you and your answer from God! Just because someone is ill, it doesn't mean they are living in sin! Elijah was made out of the same "mud" as the rest, but He believed God and His #1 motive in life was to serve God, he wasn't perfect but he confessed his sins on a regular basis and was striving to be a godly man.

We all seem to constantly be looking for some "magical formula" to prayer when the Bible makes it very clear, over and over that is our faith that moves God. There were many times when Jesus told people, "it is your faith that has made you whole" and there were places He went where He didn't perform many miracles because of their lack of faith (Matthew 13:58 ESV). Faith is believing that God will do what He has said He will do, we all know He can do anything. What if He says "no"? Then what? Does that mean you have sin in your life or He doesn't care? No! God loves you and His plan is perfect for your life and He promises to do what is right and best! We do live in an imperfect world and bad things happen to good people and there are times we make decisions that land us where we are. Things don't always change over night, but that is no reason to give up! Faith is believing that God will bring that answer or that miracle in His time and because we know that we hold on to our faith and believe and serve and follow Him as we wait! God knows what is best and that is what He is committed to!

Faith is knowing that God sees more than you do, and if He takes that person you love it may be that He is saving them from something by far worse than what you see today! As difficult as that it we have to believe that! I have lost many dear people to me over the years, including both of my parents and it is so difficult and we don't always understand the timing or reason, but God is God and we have to trust Him when He says, "My ways are not your ways, and My thoughts are not your thoughts", but we know that He is committed to what is best!

Now, we seem to have gotten away from this very important process that is mentioned in these verses above: "Is anyone among you sick? Let him call for the elders of the church, and let them pray over him, anointing him with oil in the name of the Lord. And the prayer of faith will save the one who is sick, and the Lord will raise him up." My daughter, Candace and I just had this discussion this morning! Why are we not in the practice of doing this any more? God is THE God of miracles and the God of healing! Pull together some godly people and people who are known for their faith and anoint that person and pray over them believing. If God has not told you, "no, you will not be healed" then pray, believe, anoint with oil! Satan has almost made us feel embarrassed to ask for prayer and to be anointed with oil somehow and we need to recognize his schemes and press into God and hold on to His word, believe and pray for miracles! Don't give up, no matter what the doctors may say, God can do anything! Unless He tells you it is time, then you are called to have faith and believe! Share those prayer requests with us today and take them to the elders of your church! The best is yet to come!

Quote:

*"God grant me the serenity to accept the things
I cannot change, The courage to change the things
I can, and the wisdom to know the difference."*
REINHOLD NIEBUHR

~ How Can You Apply This To Your Life Today ~

~ DAY 64 ~

ARE YOU THERE GOD

ROMANS 10:17
So faith comes from hearing, and hearing
trough the word of Christ. (ESV)

Faith! We all want more faith so the other day I asked God just exactly how are we able to have more faith? I played over in my mind all the times I would desperately "believe" for my answer to be there and 'run to the mailbox' and there's nothing, or I would work up "faith" in my mind to the point I could feel that I believed with every part of my being and ...... nothing! So, I asked...... "what's up with that?" How can I have faith, if I can't seem to believe enough to get an answer! Are you there God? Do you really care?

What am I missing? Well that was the question He was waiting for! What am I missing? He knows I know the answer to .... are you there and do you care! Hello! Of course He is there and He cares more than we can comprehend! Well, here's the answer I got:

Faith begins with trust! Do you trust Him? Really? Do you trust Him with your finances? If you said yes to that then do you tithe or do you feel as though you just can't afford to tithe? Hmmmmmm..... how about the verse that says in Luke 6:38, "Give, and it will be given to you: good measure, pressed down, shaken together, and running over will be put into your bosom. For with the same measure that you use, it will be measured back to you." Trust Him with it!

How about your marriage? Do you feel if everything doesn't quite turn out how you had planned you will never be able to live with it? How do you pray when you pray for your spouse? Do you believe that God will see you through regardless of how things turn out? If that spouse is willing to allow God to work in their life, anything is possible so pray for God to give them a willing heart and allow God to work in His way and His timing. Know that if somehow it doesn't work God will still see you through and give you the strength you need to be all you can be for Him. If you are in an abusive situation, pray for God's deliverance and allow Him to show what to you! God loves you and wants His best for you! Trust God with your children as well! The best gift you can give your children is your prayer to God for them! Don't ever give up on them, God hasn't!

Your faith will also be increased as you praise Him! Sit down and praise God for who He is! Turn on some praise and worship music and allow it to sink deep down into your heart and watch as your struggles start to appear smaller in the shadow of who your God is!

The list could go on and on from finances, marriage to your job, your health, no matter what it is that you need an answer for today, God is asking you to trust Him. Give it all to Him! Be obedient in all He asks. Spend more time in His word, getting to know Him better! Spend time praising Him for who He is and watch as your faith grows in His presence! Know that He loves you and He truly wants His best for you so trust Him today knowing that the best is yet to come!

Quote:

"It is one of the most beautiful compensations in life we can never help another without helping ourselves."
RALPH WALDO EMERSON

~ How Can You Apply This To Your Life Today ~

~ DAY 65 ~

ARE YOU A FAITH CRUSHER OR A FAITH BUILDER

MATTHEW 21: 21-22

And Jesus answered them, "Truly, I say to you, if you have faith and do not doubt, you will not only do what has been done to the fig tree, but even if you say to this mountain, 'Be taken up and thrown into the sea,' it will happen. And whatever you ask in prayer, you will receive, if you have faith." (ESV)

Are you a faith crusher or a faith builder? When you or someone else prays for something do you do you pull out every ounce of faith you can muster and ask God for the faith you lack or do you come up with little quips like, "well, I prayed, but I'm not holding my breath" or "well, I'm not really counting on it, seems like it would take a miracle"?

It only takes one faith crusher to ruin the faith of the whole group. It only takes one person to constantly plant negative thoughts to dwindle the faith of the rest. It is just like the yeast in bread that Jesus used to use as an example of the Pharisees and their poor attitudes affecting everyone around them if they were listened to for too long.

It can happen in your church, it can happen in your small group, it can happen in your home. Stop it! If it is you then I would encourage you to get on your knees and ask God to help you to guard your words about what He will or will not do and what He is capable of doing. If it is someone around you it may be time to just stop them when they start and tell them "I can't listen to that right now."

The Bible tells us that without faith it is impossible to please God. Well now, where does that leave us if we are faith crushers or we allow someone else to crush our faith?

Hold on tight to your faith today ladies! Don't allow someone to rob you of all that God has planned because they have a hideous attitude! Hold your head high, hang onto what Jesus is saying to you in these verses! Claim all that is in these verses, remind Jesus, 'this is what you said and I am believing you for it."

We still, of course need to be praying within the will of God, but you know all of that. This isn't about that it is about having faith and trusting God to do all He has said He will do. It is about reminding ourselves who we are talking to and all He has done and who He is! It is no small thing to go before God with what is on your heart. Make sure your heart is clean and your attitude is in check and that you are within the boundaries of what God would consider to be right and then hold on to your faith and believe. Don't waiver and don't allow someone else to use their words to rob you. The best is yet to come but you must choose to believe.

Quote:

"Adversity causes some people to break;
others to break records."
WILLIAM A. WARD

~ How Can You Apply This To Your Life Today ~

~ DAY 66 ~

HAVE FAITH THAT HE WILL SHINE HIS LIGHT ON YOUR SITUATION

PROVERBS 3:5-6

Trust in the Lord with all your heart, and do not lean on your own understanding,. In all your ways acknowledge him, and he will make straight your paths. (ESV)

I remember one night when my children were really little, my son was 5 and the other two were 2 1/2 years old and about 4 months. My husband was working nights so on Wednesday evenings I would catch a ride with another couple to church. One night they dropped me and the children off at home and I walked into the garage and realized I didn't have the key to get in the house and someone had locked the door going from the garage into the living room! I ran back outside to try to catch them, but they were already gone! Now, I will definitely date myself here, but we didn't have cell phones back then so I couldn't just call my "landlord" and ask him to come let me in or call the couple that just left to ask them to give me a ride to the landlord's house either which was about a half mile away. I took a look outside and it was pitch black, there were clouds covering the sky so there wasn't even a tiny star to help light the way. We lived out in the middle of no where. I knew what I was going to have to do, I was going to have to walk down that sandy, dirt road to my landlord's house with kids in tow, in high heels in pitch blackness! Before I stepped out of that garage, I prayed! I prayed for God to help me find my way, to somehow help me see where I was going and to protect us from any wild animals that could be out there as well. I started walking down the driveway, my children, quite reluctant, but holding my hands, thank God for infant carriers, and before we reached the end of the driveway, a hole opened up in the clouds and the moon shown through! I have never been so grateful to God to see the moon as I was on that night! We walked down to the landlords house and he drove us back and on the way he asked how on earth I could see to get to his house, it was pitch black out! He was a very godly man so when I told him about the moon, he just laughed and said that made sense, that God is good like that!

Are you feeling today like you are in utter darkness in your situation? Are you needing God to lead and yet the way seems completely hopeless because you just can't see how it could possibly "work out for your good"? I am here to tell you, He is able! Nothing is too difficult for Him and nothing is too small of a matter for Him to care! That moonlight was only there long enough for me to leave that driveway and to knock on their door and it was gone! Here's the deal though, the moon didn't peak through those clouds until I stepped out and trusted God to get us where we needed to go! Was I scared before I stepped out? Yes! If it were just me walking that would have been bad enough, but I had 3 small children! I had no choice but to trust God if I wanted that door unlocked. If there is a door you need unlocked in your life, it may be time to pray and step out in faith believing that He will light your way! He will give you what it takes to get to your answer! Believe Him and trust Him and get started Girl! Don't wait for His light to show up first, trust that when you need it, it will be there! Step out in faith today knowing that the best is yet to come!

Quote:

"Faith is taking the first step even when
you don't see the whole staircase."
MARTIN LUTHER KING

~ How Can You Apply This To Your Life Today ~

~ DAY 67 ~

"CRAZY FAITH"

MARK 11: 22 - 24

And Jesus answered them,"Have faith in God. Truly I say to you, whoever says to this mountain,'Be taken up and throw into the sea,' and does not doubt in his heart, but believes that what he says will come to pass, it will be done for him. Therefore I tell you, whatever you ask in prayer, believe that you have received it, and it will be yours."

Quite clearly that was Jesus talking in those verses! Question for you: Is Jesus, the Son of the Most High God, capable of lying? No! No, He is not! He is God the Son, He will not lie, it is not within His character to lie, so do you believe Him?

We struggle so much with faith. Why? Jesus got so frustrated with the lack of faith on the earth when He was here walking on the earth. He couldn't believe that the people didn't take God at His word and we don't seem to be much better at it today.

We are called to have, as my friend Dianna said yesterday, "Crazy faith"! If what you are praying for lines up with the Word of God then you need to believe! Faith is not just knowing God can, it is believing that He will do what is best for you! It is believing that He will show up when He has said He would! Now, you must also remember that when it comes to praying for other people, they do have a free will and God has given us the free will to choose. He will not force that other person any more than He will force you to do what is right and believe. If you are praying for someone else, pray for them to develop a heart that is open to His leading and also pray that He will give you the strength to continue to follow Him even if they don't. The key to praying is believing that if we knew what He knows we would be praying for what He would choose. Trust is a huge thing when it comes to relationships and that includes your relationship with God! Do you trust Him? I seem to be continually learning to trust Him more. I have been through some "scary" things in my life and let me tell you, there's really nothing else to do other than trust Him. Well, you could choose to get angry and frustrated with Him, but what purpose will the serve?

God loves you and wants His best for you. Whatever you are facing today, He wants to be there and He wants to see you through. He wants you to have faith that will move those mountains that are in front of you, standing in your way of serving Him more! His desire is for your best. Trust Him and believe Him. Don't waiver in your faith if what you are praying and believing for line up with scripture! Pray! Take your thoughts captive to ward off all doubt and believe God for what He has told you!

Seek His face! Pray without reservation, believing that He will do what He has promised. Get some 3x5 cards out or some paper and write down every scripture you can find that fits your situation or promise you feel God has given you and carry it with you and when you start to doubt, pull them out and read them! You can start with Psalm 121:1-2, "I lift up my eyes to the mountains ~ where does my help come from? My help comes from the Lord, the Maker of heaven and earth." If you are struggling with your faith, pray as the father of the child who was possessed in Mark 9: 24 did,

Immediately the father of the child cried out and said, "I believe; help my unbelief!" Let's pray today for "crazy faith"!

Quote:

"Faith believes in spite of the circumstances
and acts in spite of the consequences."
ADRIAN ROGERS

~ How Can You Apply This To Your Life Today ~

~ DAY 68 ~

YOU WILL FIND MORE FAITH WHEN YOU PRAISE HIM

1 CHRONICLES 29:11

Yours, O Lord, is the greatness and the power and the glory and the victory and the majesty, for all that is in the heavens and in the earth is yours. Yours is the kingdom, O Lord, and you are exalted as head above all. (ESV)

Let's take a day and really focus on praising God for all that He is! Praise will increase your faith beyond anything you can imagine! Praise not only blesses God that you are recognizing Him for Who He is, it reminds you of you He is!

If you go to church today, think of every word you are singing as you praise Him. Don't allow yourself to sink into auto pilot as you sing praise to Him, think about what you are saying and let it pour out from your heart! If you are not in church today as you read this, no matter what day of the week it is I would like to encourage you to turn on some praise music and sing your heart out to God praising Him for His goodness and majesty and grace!

I am sure if you take a look around today and you hear or read the news, it is disheartening at the wickedness that is going on in the world today! So much hate and despair! That is all the more reason to remind yourself of who God is! Praise Him so you will increase your faith! Praise Him to bless His heart! He knows you! He sees you and He cares about all that you are facing! Praise Him that He is a God who is faithful and He will fulfill all that He has promised! Praise Him that He will give you strength! Praise Him that He is a God who heals and a God who mends our broken hearts and carries us when we just can't make it another day due to the heartaches we bear!

The toughest thing to do when you are overwhelmed with hurt can be the thought of singing praise to God, but it is also the most healing thing. If you are hurting, pour your heart out to Him, praise Him that He sees and that He will carry you through and tell Him about all of your hurts and pains. Ask Him to help you with any anger that has been brought on by your situation and ask Him to comfort your heart! Know that He keeps track of your every tear and you matter and He is working on your behalf to see you through and to help you become all He created you to be! He loves you ~ He has heard your prayers! Please pray for others today that you know are overwhelmed and broken hearted as well!

Quote:

"Action conquers fear."
PETE ZARLENGA, *How Can You Apply This To Your Life Today*

~ How Can You Apply This To Your Life Today ~

~ DAY 69 ~

IS TODAY YOUR "PIT TO PALACE" DAY

GENESIS 40:15

For I was indeed stolen out of the land of the Hebrews, and here also I have done nothing that they should put me into the pit. (ESV)

Do you feel like no matter what, you just seem to go from one pit to the next in life?

Joseph first had to deal with his brothers throwing him in a pit and selling him to traders who were on their way to Egypt, then Potiphar's wife lied about Joseph and his character and he was sent to prison for something he didn't do. He must have felt a bit frustrated because one day he was in his father's house and had some pretty incredible dreams about his future and the next thing he knew he was just surviving going from one pit to the next. In all of this though, Joseph was faithful.

There are pits in life, it happens to everyone we just have different "pits". The key is this; it isn't about whether or not you will find yourself in a pit one day, it is how you will handle it when you do. Joseph chose to remain faithful to God no matter what and

God blessed all that he did whether he was in a pit or not. Joseph probably missed his home and his Dad but he didn't sit around wallowing in self pity he kept pressing forward doing his best in all that he did and as a result he went from this last pit to the palace!

Genesis 41: 14, "Then Pharaoh sent and called Joseph, and they brought him hastily out of the dungeon: and he shaved himself, and changed his raiment, and came in unto Pharaoh." Verse 38 says, "And Pharaoh said unto his servants, "Can we find such a one as this is, a man in whom the Spirit of God is?" 39 – 42, And Pharaoh said unto Joseph, Forasmuch as God hath showed thee all this, there is none so discreet and wise as thou art: Thou shalt be over my house, and according unto thy word shall all my people be ruled: only in the throne will I be greater than thou. And Pharaoh said unto Joseph, See, I have set thee over all the land of Egypt. And Pharaoh took off his ring from his hand, and put it upon Joseph's hand, and arrayed him in vestures of fine linen, and put a gold chain about his neck;

Don't underestimate where you are headed. God can take whatever is thrown at you and turn it into so much more than you could possibly plan or imagine! Trust Him in all that you do and spend your time growing and pressing forward no matter what. Don't be discouraged that right now you are in the "pits", grow from all that is around you and ask Him for His grace and mercy to get to the other side because you just never know when your day will come to go from that pit to the palace.

Quote:

"Beautiful light is born of darkness so the faith that springs from conflict is often the strongest and best."
R. TURNBULL

~ How Can You Apply This To Your Life Today ~

~ DAY 70 ~

HIS DESIRE IS TO INCREASE YOUR FAITH

HEBREWS 11:1-2
Now faith is the substance of things hoped
for, the evidence of things not seen. For by it
the elders obtained a good report. (KJV)

Hebrews chapter 11 is knows as the "faith" chapter and it is a great reminder of the faith these men and women of God that Paul listed had. Where is your faith today? Could you be listed as having the faith to trust all that God is doing in your life is for a purpose so you remain faithful to all you know to be true and you are hanging on to that hope for the future He has planned or are you wavering a bit today?

We all have those days, not that that makes it right, but we do all have those days when we find ourselves scratching our heads asking God, "what are you doing ~ are you still there?" It is so important when you have one of those days to stop what you are doing and spend as much time with Him as you possibly can, if there are activities or chores that can wait, let them wait and sit down and spend some time reading, praying, listening to praise and worship music, watch an encouraging preacher on tv, but don't ignore your wavering faith. In verse 6 it says, But without faith it is impossible to please Him, for he who comes to God must believe that He is, and that He is a rewarder of those who diligently seek Him." God is faithful and He has called us to be faithful to all that He calls us to.

In Mark chapter 9 one of the stories there is about a man whose son had an unclean spirit that possessed him and when Jesus told the father, "If you can believe, all things are possible to him who believes." the man cried and said, "I believe, help my unbelief" and Jesus healed the boy. What does that mean to you? Does it at least encourage you that you can go to God and say those same words, "I believe, help my unbelief!" and then watch God move in your situation! God loves you and wants to work in your life in amazing ways, He wants His glory to shine in the situation you are facing, He wants to increase your faith!

I would like to encourage you today to have the faith that God isn't finished with you yet and He is right there beside you. Ask Him today for more faith and for His strength to get you through to the other side. What you face today is temporary and He will see you through. Just like the Israelites passing through the desert before the promised land, this may be your training ground for your promised land, learn to trust Him and to obey all that He is asking you to do today and take heart knowing this is just a short season in your life ~ The best is yet to come!

Quote:

"Beautiful light is born of darkness, so the faith that
springs from conflict is often the strongest and best."
R. TURNBULL

~ How Can You Apply This To Your Life Today ~

~ DAY 71 ~

IS YOUR FAITH WAVERING

MARK 9:19

And he answered them, "O faithless generation,
how long am I to be with you? How long am I to
bear with you? Bring him to me." (ESV)

Jesus was frustrated with their lack of faith! How much did they have to see Him do in order to believe? How about you? How's your faith doing this morning? Do you believe that God wants His best for you or are you wavering in that belief today? How often do we blame God for where we are or for the lack of results in areas of our lives that we need His help in desperately and yet maybe all along the problem is really us not Him!

First of all, let's start a few verses down from this one where they said to Jesus, "But if you can do anything……" and Jesus said, "IF YOU CAN!" He had to be thinking, IF? Are they really so blind yet, that they aren't sure IF I can? Yes, they were! When you look at your situation today are you wondering IF God can do something? As Jesus said, "All things are possible for one who believes!" Nothing is impossible with God, ladies! He can do all things, He created all things, He sees all, and He cares about what you are facing!

Now, I have even tried the excuse of "but these are the only results I have ever seen....." and I instantly heard; "don't blame me for either your lack of effort or your pursuit of something that was not within my will." Ooh, ouch! Wait, what? Are you possibly saying that maybe my issues are often my own doing? Well, let's take inventory here, or maybe not; how about we just start fresh today and follow His lead and we do all that He puts in front of us "with all our might" (Ecclesiastes 9:10) and that we pray and allow Him to guide us and that we believe that He wants His best for us and have faith to believe that He is capable and will do as He has promised!

How about you? Where are you in all of this today? Is there something you are not fully believing Him for? Is your faith wavering? Trust Him, choose to have faith and believe that He will come through and do all He has promised! The best is yet to come!

Quote:

"First we make our attitudes. Then our attitudes make us."
DENNIS WAITLEY

~ How Can You Apply This To Your Life Today ~

~ DAY 72 ~

FAITH TO MOVE THAT MOUNTAIN YOU ARE FACING

MATTHEW 17:20

He said to them, "Because of your little faith. For truly, I say to you, if you have faith like a grain of mustard seed, you will say to this mountain, 'Move from here to there,' and it will move, and nothing will be impossible for you." (ESV)

What mountains are you facing today? Are there things that you are facing financially or in your relationships, your health or maybe your walk with Christ that seem impossible to overcome? Do you truly believe this verse? Nothing is impossible for you if you just believe and you are walking in the will of God. In this verse Jesus was talking to the disciples about why they couldn't cast out demons that He could and He was explaining that it was their lack of faith. Where are you lacking in faith? I know my weakest faith moments often come with our finances, maybe that is why we keep facing the same issues over and over – God is trying to increase my faith!

The Bible says in Hebrews 11:6 "And without faith it is impossible to please him, for whoever would draw near to God must believe that he exists and that he rewards those who seek him." If we want

God to move on our behalf then it is imperative that we choose to believe that He is stronger and bigger than whatever mountain is in our way! God is able and willing to deliver so we need to believe and have the faith necessary to move that mountain. We all know that a mustard seed is the tiniest seed so God is not asking for a mountain of faith to move a tiny seed He is asking for a tiny amount of faith to move that huge mountain in our lives.

Ask God today for the faith you need and the wisdom to know if there is anything else that you need to recognize that is holding you back from moving that mountain in your life. God's desire is for you to have victory in your life on every level, He is ready and willing to help you overcome your mountains today! Let's all move forward into the new Year asking God to increase our faith in every area of our lives!

Quote:

"Life begins when you do."
HUGH DOWNS

~ How Can You Apply This To Your Life Today ~

~ DAY 73 ~

GROW YOUR FAITH BY REMINDING YOURSELF OF WHO HE IS

ROMANS 4:20

*No distrust made him waver concerning the
promise of God, but he grew strong in his faith
as he gave glory to God, fully convinced that God
was able to do what he had promised. (ESV)*

How are you doing today on the scales of Faith? Are you wavering a bit or are you trusting and fully believing that God will come through?

I remember when I was little hearing the verse: Matthew 17:20 that says, So Jesus said to them, "….. for assuredly, I say to you, if you have faith as a mustard seed, you will say to this mountain,, 'Move from here to there,' and it will move; and nothing will be impossible for you." Well, that sounded simple enough so I headed out to the back yard and was determined to see that hill out back moved! I wasn't sure what we were going to do if it was gone, but I wanted to see it happen! If it had moved, I may have been a bit disappointed in the winter because that was my favorite place to go sledding, but hey….. I would have found a way to get over it I guess! Who didn't think that as a kid? I think it may have done something to my faith basket though, somehow I took that lack of 'movement' as acknowledgement that I just didn't have enough faith, or maybe I just wasn't important enough to God, maybe getting prayers answered was just for other 'more important' people!

I have really been praying that God would teach me more about faith and what I needed to do in order to develop my faith. There are are so many verses in the Bible on Faith we could just sit and read them for hours. I have been praying like the man in Mark 9:24, Immediately the father of the child cried out and said with tears, "Lord, I believe; help my unbelief!" As I have been praying that over the last several months I have been amazed at the simple things He has shown me!

We all know that Abraham was a man of faith, but where did that faith come from: Romans 4:20- 21 tells us about Abraham and his faith, it says, "No distrust made him waver concerning the promise of God, but he grew strong in his faith as he gave glory to God, fully convinced that God was able to do what he had promised.

Our faith is directly connected to our praise! The more we remind ourselves of who God is and how He sees us, the more we believe! The more our faith grows!

I have been reading a lot about David including Psalms; I have always been impressed with how he was considered a 'man after god's own heart' and I wondered why. What made God consider Him a man after his own heart, it isn't like David was perfect by any means so what was it? David was constantly consumed with Who God Is! He would pour his heart out to God in prayer begging God to slay his enemies and then in the middle of it all he would pour his heart out in praise of who God is and all that God had done already for him and for Israel.

We need to spend more time praising God and recognizing who He is! We need to spend time just thanking Him and praising Him for all He has done! The more we focus on Him, the more faith we have because we realize more and more that that Huge Mountain of a problem is just a little thing to Him!

Without Faith it is impossible to please God, Hebrews 11:6, that could very well be because it means we are not recognizing Him for all that He is! God is a great God and there's just nothing that He can't do! He loves us and the more faith we have in Who He is the more we will trust Him and love Him! That's the best place to be!

I would like to encourage you today to start praising Him and thanking Him for all He is, all He has done and all He is going to do in your life! Spend some serious time dwelling on Him and your faith will grow!

Quote:

"It's not the things you get but the hearts you touch
that will determine your success in life."
SIMPLE TRUTHS *www.simpletruths.com*

~ How Can You Apply This To Your Life Today ~

~ DAY 74 ~

IS FAITH OR FEAR RULING YOUR DAY

ROMANS 1: 16-17

For I am not ashamed of the gospel of Christ, for it is the power of God for salvation to everyone who believes, for the Jew first and also for the Greek. For in it the righteousness of God is revealed from faith to faith; as it is written, "The just shall live by faith." (NKJV)

Which one is ruling in your heart today; faith or fear? I am by no means saying that in a condemning way because let me tell you, with everything that is going on in the world today it is understandable that fear is running rampant even among believers. We are living in a day when not only has "wrong become right" but now it is "wrong" if you believe in what the Bible tells us is right because you may offend someone! It is a scary place when we aren't even just told to be tolerant of sin we are told that if we say anything against sin we are the ones who are in the wrong! That is just so messed up! But, even though the world has gone crazy, we can still have faith in God because He is still on the throne!

The Bible is full of God's promises and all of the stories of His faithfulness! He has promised in His word to always do what is best. He has promised you that He has a plan, Jeremiah 29:11, "For I know the plans I have for you," declares the Lord, "plans to prosper you and not to harm you, plans to give you hope and a future." (NIV) Hold on to that hope and allow Him to guide you to the future He has planned for your life!

We all know that the opposite of faith is fear but do we understand that there is one thing they have in common? "Faith and Fear both believe in a future that hasn't happened yet!" (John Gordon) How true is that? Have you ever stopped to think about that thing you fear the most, and made yourself recognize the fact that you are just supposing what may happen. There is no truth in it yet because it hasn't happened yet so in a sense you are spending your time worrying about your imagination. I catch myself doing that all the time; you hear something that has happened to someone else and the next thing you know you find yourself so consumed with the fear of that happening to you that you can't function on the level God has called you to. Stop putting yourself in other people's shoes ~ God didn't fit you with the grace to wear them! God gives us grace and strength to deal with situations when they happen to us, not before, not just after and certainly not when it has happened to someone else instead of us! You get your own grace from God for your "stuff" not everyone else's.

God wants you to walk in the confidence and faith for your life that He is still God and He is in control! Not one hair is going to fall out of your head that He doesn't know about. He loves you and nothing can happen to you that won't pass by Him first. Trust Him! Pray! Spend time in prayer over all those things that are concerning you! Instead of allowing them to consume you and immobilize you, take them to Him and leave them there. Ask Him to consume you with His peace and strength! Find a group of faith filled people to spend some time with as it says in Romans 1:12…"that we may be mutually encouraged by each others faith, both yours and mine." Our faith is meant to encourage each other. Hold on to your faith and Hope in Him ~ the best is yet to come!

Quote:

"The bridges you cross before you come to them are over rivers that aren't there."
GENE BROWN

~ How Can You Apply This To Your Life Today ~

~ DAY 75 ~

REMIND YOURSELF OF ALL HE HAS DONE

1 CHRONICLES 16:34
O give thanks unto the Lord; for he is good; for his steadfast love endures forever! (ESV)

What are you thankful for today? Or, maybe I should be asking; are you thankful today for something or are you focused on what you wish you had or what you wish would happen. We really need to choose everyday to be more thankful for all God has done and all He has given us! God is so good!

I know that after being in Africa, I am thankful for a bathroom and clean water! Take a look around today though and really stop and thank God for what He has done for you. We spend so much time praying for what we need or want that we seem to forget to spend the time we should just being grateful. Taking the time to be grateful to God for all He has done will increase your faith!

If you focus on what you don't have you will never be happy! Focus today on what you do have, take the time to focus on all that God has done, not on what you are waiting on. The next time you feel that urge to look down on someone else that doesn't have much compared to you, humble yourself and thank God for what all He has done for you and pray for blessing on that other person.

I would encourage you to go beyond just being thankful for material things and even health but look at the mercy and grace God has shown you over the years. Take some time to reflect on the price He paid for your sins so you could be free to move forward in life, take the time to think about His grace that has carried you through tough times, take the time to think about the people He has put in your life over the years that have helped, really take the time to think on all He has done and thank Him for it today!

Ladies, let's take today and be thankful for all that God has done for us, let's just for today set aside what we are frustrated over and think on all that is good in our lives. Thank God for His grace, mercy and love and focus on what a powerful, awesome and gracious God He is!

Quote:

"Until you make peace with who you are you will never be content with what you have."
DORIS MORTMAN

~ How Can You Apply This To Your Life Today ~

~ DAY 76 ~

HOLD ON TO HIS PROMISES

NUMBERS 14:1 AND 4
Then all the congregation raised a loud cry, and the people
wept that night.....
And they said to one another, "Let us choose
a leader and go back to Egypt." (ESV)

The spies that Moses had sent out to check out the promised land had just come back and had given a negative report of what the people would face going in to the land. Joshua and Caleb tried to convince the people that with God's help they could take the land, just like God said they would. After seeing all the miracles God had done for them since He brought them out of Egypt, they still had no faith that He would drive the people of the land out like He promised!

We can wonder what their problem was and we have pretty good insight to what we would tell them if given the chance, but that is because we can see the full picture. But what about you? Is there something you know God has given you to do but you are allowing fear to keep you from all He has for you? Is there a business opportunity or new job that you are so afraid of failing at that you won't do what you need to do to be successful? Is there a relationship that needs to be restored in your life? Are you facing a mountain of illness or addiction that you just don't see a way through to the other side? Don't allow fear to consume your faith! Hold on to the promises of God! Until you get a "NO" from Him, if you believe you are within His will then believe for His best and move with confidence toward that!

There are always going to be battles in life and struggles that can overwhelm, but if you know you are doing the will of God, then rest assured that you are not alone and He didn't bring you to this point to fail. Trust Him! Look for His best, pray for His favor and for Him to bring the right people into your life! Don't run! Hold on to His promises, remember Jeremiah 29:11, "For I know the plans I have for you," declares the Lord, "plans to prosper you and not to harm you, plans to give you hope and a future." (NIV) Carry that verse with you, pull it out when you need to be reminded and trust Him that the best is yet to come!

Quote:

"Attitude is a little thing that makes a big difference."
SIMPLE TRUTHS *www.simpletruths.com*

~ How Can You Apply This To Your Life Today ~

~ DAY 77 ~

NO DOUBTING TODAY

MATTHEW 21:21-22

And Jesus answered them, "Truly, I say to you, if
you have faith and do not doubt, you will not only
do what has been done to the fig tree, but even if you
say to this mountain, 'be taken up and thrown into
the sea,' it will happen. And whatever you ask in
prayer you will receive, if you have faith." (ESV)

Remember the story of when I was a little girl how amazed I was when I heard these verses in Sunday school? I was still at an age where I took everything quite literally and I was determined that I had enough faith to have that hill moved from Northern Michigan to the ocean! Well, sometimes, as adults I think we still look at this verse and see it the same way. If we ask and have faith then it is going to happen, we don't stop to think about how it will affect the world around us, other people and whether or not we are operating with Matthew 6:33 in mind, "But seek ye first the kingdom of God, and his righteousness; and all these things shall be added unto you." Are you seeking the will of God for your life, are you putting Him first? If we put God first and we truly seek Him and His will then our desires will line up with His and then we can have the faith that He will hear our prayers and we can have the faith to believe that all that He does in our lives and for us is for our best!

We need to be obedient and have faith that we are the children of the Most High God and He loves us and His desire is to bless us and give us His favor. He wants to show the world Who He is through you!

I don't know what Mountain you are facing today but if you trust Him He can move it for you. I love this old song from FFH called "Lord Move or Move Me" Back when the song first came out I had a serious situation that I needed God to move in and this song meant a lot to me. It didn't happen overnight but when He moved, He moved me and it was amazing how all the pieces came together! God hears your prayers and He has a plan. Trust Him to do what is best. Remember, if we knew what He knows we would ask for what He is about to give us!

Don't allow your faith to waiver today! Hold on to your hope only found in Him!

Quote:

*"Faith is knowing there is an ocean
because you have seen a brook."*
WILLIAM ARTHUR WARD

~ How Can You Apply This To Your Life Today ~

~ DAY 78 ~

NOTHING IS TOO DIFFICULT FOR HIM

PSALM 100:3

Know ye that the Lord he is God: it is he that hath made us, and not we ourselves; we are his people, and the sheep of his pasture. (KJV)

We need to know! We need to know deep within our hearts that the Lord is God! That may sound simple and strange to say, but how much more faith would we have in our every day lives if we would really dig in and fully grasp that the Lord that we pray to is God of all. We often take it all for granted and so lightly that we forget who we are talking to when we pray and we forget in our struggle that He can handle whatever may come our way! He is God! He is Lord of All! Nothing is too difficult for Him, He made it all!

If you are hurting today, your heart is wounded or grieving ~ Know that the God of all, the Lord, He is God and He cares and will mend your heart. If you are lonely ~ know that the Lord, He is God and He is right by your side, He can fill your heart with joy and can bring people into your life to fill the void again. If you are struggling in your finances or your marriage ~ know that the Lord,

He is God and nothing is too difficult for Him, if you follow Him, He will show you the way and He will provide for you! No matter what it is that you need today ~ know that the Lord, He is God and He is working on your situation and in your life and He cares more deeply than you can possibly fathom! He loves you!

No matter what may come your way today, no matter what thoughts cross your mind, keep reminding yourself "the Lord, He is God" and He cares and He will see me through to the other side of all of this! The best is yet to come!

Quote:

"Do what you can with what you have, where you are!"
THEODORE ROOSEVELT

~ How Can You Apply This To Your Life Today ~

~ DAY 79 ~

HE IS FAITHFUL AND HE WILL SEE YOU THROUGH

2 THESSALONIANS 3:3
But the Lord is faithful. He will establish you and guard you against the evil one. (ESV)

Is there a daunting task in front of you that has you almost paralyzed with fear of stepping out in faith? Has satan been taunting you, making you feel as though there is just no way you can or should do what God seems to be calling you to?

God is faithful and if He is leading you into something, He will see you through! He won't ask you to do something and then leave you hanging if you are truly following Him! Remember, satan is the father of lies and he hates you! He will do his best to discourage you and make you feel like you are alone to keep you from following God's plan because God's plan is always to lead you into His best for your life! He often even tries to twist scripture, to hold you back or discourage you!

If you want to truly feel established and secure then you have to trust God with all that He is putting before you? Remember Joshua 1:9, "Have I not commanded you? Be strong and courageous. Do not be frightened, and do not be dismayed, for the Lord your God is with you wherever you go." Just as God was with Joshua, He will be with you in what He is asking you to do! You serve the same God and He is faithful! Don't allow satan to fill your head with lies! Pray for God to constantly reveal the truth to you and to guide you so you don't make a mistake! He loves you and wants you to succeed in all that He created you to do, so trust Him!

If it seems like a tremendous leap of faith to step out, but you know that this is what He is calling you to do, then jump! Go after it with all you've got! Don't hold anything back! Have you ever watched a small child jump into their Dad's arms in a pool? Jump with that kind of faith, knowing He's got you and He isn't going to let you fall! Pour yourself into His word and ask Him to guide your every step and then rest in Him, knowing that He will get you through this, struggles and all and you will be so much better for it on the other side! His best is yet to come! It's worth the fight. We all want to think that His best is going to just fall into our laps, but in most cases, we have to strive for what is good and right, but you don't have to do it alone! He's got you and He will give you the right people to walk with you through this if you just ask!

Quote:

"Whether you think you can, or think you can't..... you are right."
HENRY FORD

~ How Can You Apply This To Your Life Today ~

~ DAY 80 ~

WHAT WILL IT TAKE TO GROW YOUR FAITH

MATTHEW 13:58
*And he did not do many mighty works there
because of their unbelief. (ESV)*

Is there something you need or maybe want? Take a look at Peter in Matthew 14 he just wanted to walk on the water like Jesus, was it necessary? No. But, God knew it would increase His faith, what do you think God could want to give you that would also increase your faith? For me years ago it was a frozen pizza. Then we look at verse 31 in chapter 14 and we see that Peter took his eyes off Jesus and started looking at his immediate circumstances and he started to sink. Jesus response was to grab him and to say, "Oh you of little faith, why did you doubt?" What is He saying that to you about? Is there something just around the corner that you are about to give up on? Ask God for a verse when you have your devotions and then cling to that verse every time you start to doubt.

Somehow I feel as if we are missing out on God doing mighty works in our lives and that really saddens me! I don't want to miss out and I am sure you don't either! The people that saw Jesus walking down the street knew if they could just touch the hem of his clothes they believed they would be healed. What they didn't know was that they didn't even have to touch him it was their belief in Him and His ability to heal that healed them.

If God hasn't somehow told you "no", then believe for your answer until He moves in your situation or tells you "no". Ask Him for a verse to cling to during your moments of doubt and when you lack the faith you need today ask like the Father of the child that needed healing in Mark 9 "I believe, help my unbelief!"

Matthew 18:19 If two of you shall agree on earth as touching any thing that they shall ask, it shall be done for them of my Father who is in heaven. I am praying for you today that your faith will increase in whatever it is that you need or desire and that God will bless you beyond measure, that He will bind Satan in any area He is working on in your life and that God will have complete victory in every area you surrender to Him today. I am praying too that you will be full of Hope and that God will give you faith beyond measure and that He will do mighty things in your life. I ask that you would please pray the same for me today as well!

Quote:

"If what you believe doesn't affect how you live, then it isn't very important."
DICK NOGLEBERG

~ How Can You Apply This To Your Life Today ~

~ DAY 81 ~

WILL HE ACTUALLY COME THROUGH

PROVERBS 3:5-6

Trust in the Lord with all thine heart; and lean not unto thine own understanding. In all thy ways acknowledge him and he shall direct thy paths. (KJV)

I have found that our faith doesn't come down to whether or not we believe God can do something, it is whether or not we believe He will do it! We all know that God can do anything, after all He created everything, so we understand that nothing is to difficult for Him!

In order to grow our faith, we have to grow our trust in Him! We have to believe that if He doesn't move that mountain, there is a better plan but above that we have to believe that if the mountain needs moving, He will certainly move it!

How much do you trust Him? Let me ask you this; if you find that your finances are so backward this payday that you owe way more than what came in, do you tithe or do you feel as though you can't afford to tithe? Do you trust Him that if you are obedient He will come through and take care of all that He has promised to do? There are so many things in life that can be overwhelming and we are tempted to want to have complete control, for example; our children's lives, wouldn't it be nice if you could control all that happens so they wouldn't experience hurt and pain, but we aren't in control, so we have to learn to trust God. There are times when all of the "programs" in the world won't give you control over your finances. Life as we know it just isn't perfect in this world so your trust has to be placed in something. Are you putting your trust in Him or are you trying to hold on to control? We don't know what God knows and we certainly cannot do what God does so why do we try to hold on to control?

We must start today to hold on to Him and who He is! Get to know His heart better so you can fully understand who He is. His love is overwhelming and His goodness stretches far beyond anything we really know! Be intentional in placing your trust in Him! Your faith will grow as you learn to trust Him more!

Quote:

"Courage is a door that can only be opened from the inside."
TERRY NEIL

~ How Can You Apply This To Your Life Today ~

~ DAY 82 ~

REMAIN FAITHFUL THROUGH THE STRUGGLE

PSALM 37: 3

*Trust in the Lord, and do good; dwell in the
land and befriend faithfulness. (ESV)*

We often jump to the next verse which is also a verse that I love; "Delight yourself in the Lord, and He will give you the desires of your heart." but we need to remember that we are called to be faithful in all that we do, not just seek the "desires of our heart".

No matter what we are facing today and I know that pretty much everyone has something that they are struggling with on some level whether it is finances, relationship problems, sin or maybe health issues, we need to choose to feed on faithfulness! It is so easy and typical human nature to get to a point in the struggle where we want to just lash out because it is angering to wait for things to change or work out, but that is when we really need to press into God and fully rely on Him, trust Him and continue to do what is right and allow your heart to be filled with faithfulness to Him. We just think that the easy way out is to say, "you know what? Forget it! I am done trying to do what is right because nothing is going right and nothing is changing!" Feeling that way versus acting on it are two different things because the outcome of acting on those ideas would be destructive.

Choose to be faithful today no matter what you are facing! God is the answer ~ the only answer and He hasn't forgotten you! He is working even if you can't see it! God loves you and He will be faithful because that is who He is! If you are hurting and frustrated today because of what is going on in your life, I would like to encourage you to give it back to God because obviously you have picked it back up and you are trying to work it out on your own again! Give it to Him, ask Him for His strength and His answers, He does want to help but you have to quit trying to "fix it" yourself. Remain faithful, don't allow Satan's lies to discourage you because that is exactly what they are ~ lies!

God is the god of all and as much as He wants to help you and those around you, you must always remember; He will no more make those other people change than He will you! God does not force His plans on us, He doesn't force us to be faithful, He does ask us to trust Him though! We must remember that we can trust Him with the outcome and that means that if you fully trust Him then you know that no matter what comes your way, no matter how this turns out, God will give you the strength and blessing you need in your life to face it. The best is yet to come, trust Him for it and be faithful!

Quote:

"Reputation is what others think about you;
character is what God knows about you."
ADRIAN ROGERS

~ How Can You Apply This To Your Life Today ~

~ DAY 83 ~

YOUR SELF TALK WILL AFFECT THE OUTCOME

MATTHEW 8:8

*But the centurion replied, "Lord, I am not worthy
to have you come under my roof, but only say the
word, and my servant will be healed." (ESV)*

This man knew that there was nothing he could do to even be worthy of being in Jesus presence but he also recognized that Jesus was capable of anything. He had incredible faith! Where is your faith this morning? It is when you are in your darkest moments in life that you really need to pray and have faith in God that He will heal you and your situation. Whether it is physical healing you need or a broken heart that needs mending or your finances need healing, or relationships, or your children, whatever it is, God can fix it. Faith in God is one of the single most important things in your situation.

Our words can affect that process because our minds are powerful things! Your body will listen to the simplest suggestion that are put in your mind so we must guard our hearts and minds at all times. I was thinking about all of the crazy diets I have tried over the years and I was laughing because back in the day I had tried that crazy diet where all you do is eat this vegetable, cabbage soup and drink water for 10 days and you were supposed to lose 10 lbs! I was so excited and so faithful on that diet and I didn't weigh myself all week because I didn't want to get discouraged if it wasn't happening fast enough. Finally that last day came and I got on the scales and to my horror I had gained 10 lbs. Ladies your mind is a powerful thing and mine had decided that due to the lack of nutrition in all of my fad diets it needed to hang onto everything I ate because it figured I must be in a land of famine! If that could happen without my making negative statements about myself then just exactly what do you think can happen if you confirm negative thoughts about yourself and your situation by speaking them!

I don't know what type of healing you need today, or what kind of answers you are waiting on, but I do know that we serve a mighty God who can handle anything! He loves you and wants to help you on every level. Take the time today and thank Him for who He is and for the power He has in and over your life!

Quote:

"If you want to know where you will be in five years listen to what you are saying to yourself."
MAC ANDERSON

~ How Can You Apply This To Your Life Today ~

~ DAY 84 ~

DO YOU NEED SOME CLARITY TO BOOST YOUR FAITH

PSALM 119:143-144
Trouble and anguish have found me out, but
your commandments are my delight. Your
testimonies are righteous forever; give me
understanding that I may live. (ESV)

Do you need some clarity for what God is doing in your life right now? Do you feel as though truly trouble and anguish have found you, not only has it found you but it has run you over? Ask God to show you what you need to know and to give you understanding so you can "live" again.

God has a purpose for even the most crazy things that go on in your life when you are following Him. You may feel as though this is the worst day of your life and yet it may be what it is going to take to bring everything together so don't lose hope now. It is 'darkest before the dawn' so if it seems to be worse than anything you have seen so far your answer must be closer than you think.

Hold on to Jeremiah 29:11 today and trust that all that God says in His word is true, "For I know the plans I have for you," declares the Lord, "plans for good and not for evil to give you a future and a hope." Hold onto those words! They are meant for you! God loves you and He didn't bring you to this point or place to leave you on your own or to bring you harm, He wants you to have hope and He wants you to trust Hm to use you to the best of your ability that He has created in you!

Remind yourself as the Psalmist did here of God's goodness – "your testimonies are righteous forever" and then press forward today asking for His understanding of your situation. God has promised to reveal to us things we don't know and understand so ask when you need His wisdom for all the things you don't get. Jeremiah 33:3 says, "call to me, and I will answer you and show you great and mighty things, which you do not know." This may not have necessarily been God's plan but if He has allowed it He will also use it for His and Your good! The best is yet to come.

Quote:

"Courage is the decision to place your dreams above your fears."
ANONYMOUS

~ How Can You Apply This To Your Life Today ~

~ DAY 85 ~

DON'T LOSE SLEEP OVER IT

ROMANS 10:17
*So faith comes from hearing and hearing
through the Word of God. (ESV)*

Have you been up half the night worrying about something lately? You may not think your faith is wavering but if you are that worried about something then trust me, your faith is lacking. I have been there and I have had to lay in bed reminding myself of the verse, Isaiah 26:3, "You keep him in perfect peace whose mind is stayed on you, because he trusts in you." (ESV) That has been a great help to me when I wake up and my mind starts trying to sort something out, trying to fix it in my mind or fret over it until I am wide awake and worthless all day.

It does us no good to waste sleep at night or time during the day worrying over anything. If you have done what you can then you really need to leave the rest to God. At the point where you have done all you can, God will take care of the rest, don't get in the way with your wavering faith still trying to figure it out. "And without faith it is impossible to please him, for whoever would draw near to God must believe that he exists and that he rewards those who seek him." Hebrews 11:6. Jesus was willing to die on the cross for you, do you think His caring stopped there? Of course not, He loves you and cares about every detail of your life!

Take all that you face to God, both big and small and trust Him to do what is best for your life and the lives of those you love. James 1:6-7 says, "But let him ask in faith, with no doubting, for he who doubts is like a wave of the sea driven and tossed by the wind.. For let not that man suppose that he will receive anything from the Lord; he is a double-minded man, unstable in all his ways." Do you believe God for what He says in His word? Trust Him with your whole heart to always do what is best. When things don't turn out quite like you thought, you must still remember and understand that if you knew what He knows you would have asked for what He is doing in your life, even when things get tough.

Quote:

""Wherever you go….. go there with all your heart."
ANONYMOUS

~ How Can You Apply This To Your Life Today ~

~ DAY 86 ~

TIRED OF WAITING ~ HOLD ON TO YOUR FAITH

PSALM 69:3
I am weary with my crying out my throat is parched.
My eyes grow dim with waiting for my God.

PSALM 69:30
I will praise the name of God with a song; I will
magnify him with thanksgiving. (ESV)

Are you waiting on God for something today and you are so weary of waiting on Him that you could just scream? It seems as though at times when you wait on God for something that the days get longer and longer until you start to doubt and Satan pounces in with all of his lies saying that God doesn't care or God isn't listening ~ don't buy it!

If there is one thing David is known for above all else it is the fact that God called him a "man after God's own heart". Why do you think that is? David was a man that had so much bloodshed in his lifetime that he wasn't allowed to build the temple, he was given the instructions for his son Solomon to do it. He took another man's wife and had the man killed....... why was he called a man after God's heart?

Have you ever read the book of Psalms? No, I mean really read it, not just the skim over it kind of reading where you read, "blah, blah, blah, ... praise Him with harp and lyre.... Selah. I mean, have you ever really read the Psalms and thought about what was going on when they were written and what was being said? It is amazing how real David was with God! One minute David is saying, "oh Lord, this is horrible, everyone including my brothers are out to kill me, I can't take any more, my tears water my pillow all night, my throat is parched because of my crying and I am sick of waiting...... I will praise the Lord, my God, for all of His wondrous works, I will tell everyone of all of your great deeds, I will praise you all day long because you are so amazing, by the way.... kill all those who are coming after me, destroy them to the ends of the earth, let them be eaten by the dogs and birds of the field..... I will praise you until I am old and in the grave............

David loved God so much and He never doubted God's goodness or His love to the point that no matter what He was facing and no matter how tired He was of waiting on God, he constantly reminded himself and God that He knew God was wonderful, all powerful, able to deliver him and able to pour out revenge on David's enemies. David, would interrupt himself to say how great God is and how wonderful God had always been to his people. He would remind himself of all the great things God had done for Israel and for David. His faith came from totally trusting God in all that He faced. He went to God for everything and never hesitated to be totally honest with where he was and yet showed God the honor due Him by praising and thanking Him continually.

Walking out your faith requires you to remind yourself during the struggle who God is, what He has done and all He has promised to do.

One of the other reasons I believe that David was a man after God's own heart was because when confronted with sin in his life David "owned it" and repented. We can't just skip around the truth when it comes to any sin in our lives. Jesus paid the price on the cross for our sins the least we can do is show enough respect for Him to be repentant when we know we have sinned.

If you want to have a heart after God then pour your heart out to Him, tell Him all of your troubles and frustrations like you would your best friend, but take the time in the middle of all of that to remind yourself of Who you are talking to and praise and thank Him for Who He is, what He has done and all that He will do in your life. Remind yourself continuously of how great God is and praise Him for how Holy, Mighty and Wonderful He is. Allow your main focus to be on Him and Who He is, expect Him to care, be real in your walk with Him. Own your own sin and repent! Love God with your whole heart and know that He loves you more than you can comprehend! The world is too full of mamby, pamby Christians, my challenge to you today is to Get Real in your walk with Him!

Quote:

*"Men are anxious to improve their circumstances,
but are unwilling to improve themselves;
they therefore remain bound."*
JAMES ALLEN, *As a Man Thinketh*

~ How Can You Apply This To Your Life Today ~

~ DAY 87 ~

JUST WHEN YOU THINK THERE'S NO WAY

2 THESSALONIANS 3:3
*But the Lord is faithful. He will establish you
and guard you against the evil one.*

Is there a daunting task in front of you that has you almost paralyzed with fear of stepping out in faith? Has satan been taunting you, making you feel as though there is just no way you can or should do what God seems to be calling you to?

God is faithful and if He is leading you into something, He will see you through! He won't ask you to do something and then leave you hanging if you are truly following Him! Remember, satan is the father of lies and he hates you! He will do his best to discourage you and make you feel like you are alone to keep you from following God's plan because God's plan is always to lead you into His best for your life! He often even tries to twist scripture, to hold you back or discourage you!

If you want to truly feel established and secure then you have to trust God with all that He is putting before you? Remember Joshua 1:9, "Have I not commanded you? Be strong and courageous. Do not be frightened, and do not be dismayed, for the Lord your God is with you wherever you go." Just as God was with Joshua, He will be with you in what He is asking you to do! You serve the same God and He is faithful! Don't allow satan to fill your head with lies! Pray for God to constantly reveal the truth to you and to guide you so you don't make a mistake! He loves you and wants you to succeed in all that He created you to do, so trust Him!

If it seems like a tremendous leap of faith to step out, but you know that this is what He is calling you to do, then jump! Go after it with all you've got! Don't hold anything back! Have you ever watched a small child jump into their Dad's arms in a pool? Jump with that kind of faith, knowing He's got you and He isn't going to let you fall! Pour yourself into His word and ask Him to guide your every step and then rest in Him, knowing that He will get you through this, struggles and all and you will be so much better for it on the other side! His best is yet to come! It's worth the fight. We all want to think that His best is going to just fall into our laps, but in most cases, we have to strive for what is good and right, but you don't have to do it alone! He's got you and He will give you the right people to walk with you through this if you just ask!

Quote:

"Defeat should never be a source of discouragement,
but rather a fresh stimulus."
ROBERT SOUTH

~ How Can You Apply This To Your Life Today ~

~ DAY 88 ~

DO THE ODDS SEEM OVERWHELMING

GENESIS 18:14A

"Is anything too hard for the Lord? (ESV)

Well now, that is a good question when you feel as though you are facing overwhelming odds and you can't seem to see any way through. That question is very comforting and yet can be disturbing if you aren't fully grasping that "no, nothing is too difficult for God!" It is also a great question to ask yourself when you know God has called you to something that scares you to death! If God has called you to do something He will prepare the way and He will see you through. It all comes down to how much you trust Him!

"Ah, Lord God! It is you who have made the heavens and the earth by your great power and by your outstretched arm! Nothing is too hard for you." Jeremiah 32:17 He is the God of all, the only God and the God of all creation, how could we possibly think that anything could be too difficult for Him?

I believe what our faith really comes down to is often not whether or not we believe He can do it but more of whether or not we think He will do it! Look at the people in the Bible who came to

Jesus to be healed; they didn't come to Him because they somehow thought they deserved it ~ they came to Him because they knew He could do it so they just believed that if He can, He will and I need to be healed! They came to Jesus with humble hearts, that is obvious because often His response was, your sins have been forgiven and then they were healed of whatever their ailment was! Not all illnesses and or problems are there because of sin, some may be, some aren't but no matter why they are there, God is able to heal, God is able to help with your marriage or your finances, He wants your children to come back to Him more than you do! We need to learn to trust Him more so we will fully grasp that He has our best interest at heart and He will do what is best and right. God speaks in Jeremiah 32:27 and confirms the statement, "Behold, I am the Lord, the God of all flesh. Is anything too hard for me?"

Matthew 6:33, "But seek first the kingdom of God and His righteousness, and all these things shall be added to you." Line yourself up with what God has to say about you and all that you are facing or that He has called you to and then your faith will grow into the fact that you can trust Him and you know beyond a shadow of a doubt He can do it. God cares about even the tiniest details of your life ~ He is a God of details, just take a look around you! Ask Him to help you to grow in your walk with Him, increasing your faith and trust in Him for all that you do from this day on! The best is yet to come!

Quote:

"Unless you try to do something beyond what you have already mastered, you will never grow."
RONALD E. OSBORN

~ How Can You Apply This To Your Life Today ~

~ DAY 89 ~

TRUST AND FAITH WALK HAND IN HAND

ISAIAH 49:23B
*Then you will know that I am the Lord, those
who wait for me shall not be put to shame.*

Are you having a difficult time waiting? You know God is moving and change is about to happen but you have no idea what it is or when it might come to pass even though you know there are time frames that have to be met and as a result, you are about to pull your hair out because of the anxiety you are feeling inside. It is hard to deal with the frustrations at times when you know God has it all under control but you just wish you had a little clue what was about to happen and when. Trust me, I know exactly how that is!

If you will wait on Him and fully trust Him, He will bring it all to pass! He loves you and will not allow you to be put to shame for having trusted Him. If you allow Him to lead you now while you can't see what is next He will bring everything about in such a way that everyone will know that it is Him! His glory will shine through your answers and your future if you just wait on Him and trust Him to show you in His time.

I have to admit that there are days that I get frustrated waiting and it takes everything in me to keep it together and not allow satan to take over my thoughts. He just loves to attack during our times of trusting and waiting to fill our heads with all kinds of doubts about what God has planned; does He really have a plan, have you missed the plan, is the plan really for your good, are you sure you are hearing from God! All of those little nagging thoughts satan tries to fill your mind with will eat away at your faith if you allow them to. As soon as you get a thought like that reject it and focus on God, knowing that God always has our best interest in His mind.

If you are struggling today I would encourage you to know that God knows your deadlines too and He has a plan and He will bring it to pass so you can relax and trust Him and focus on what you need to do instead of wasting time worrying about the details He is already working on. You will be amazed as you watch God's plan unfold in front of your eyes if you will just trust Him! Know that He cares and He didn't bring you to this point to allow you to fail, He brought you to this point to do great things through you! The best is yet to come! Hang on!

Quote:

"Optimism is the faith that leads to achievement. Nothing can be done without hope and confidence."
HELEN KELLER

~ How Can You Apply This To Your Life Today ~

~ DAY 90 ~

CHOOSING DAILY TO LIVE WITH HIM WILL INCREASE YOUR FAITH

PSALM 91:1-6

He who dwells in the shelter of the Most High will abide in the shadow of the Almighty. I will say to the Lord, "My refuge and my fortress, my God, in whom I trust." For He will deliver you from the snare of the fowler and from the deadly pestilence. He will cover you with his pinions, and under his wings you will find refuge; his faithfulness is a shield and buckler. You will not fear the terror of the night nor the arrow that flies by day, nor the pestilence that stalks in darkness nor the destruction that wastes at noonday. (ESV)

Is it possible to live without fear, anxiety and frustration in our everyday lives? Who lives that way? Well, the first verses in this chapter say: "He who dwells in the shelter of the Most High will abide in the shadow of the Almighty."

If you are struggling today with fear and anxiety about life, please don't think I am making light of it! Trust me, I have been there! Some anxiety can be a physical problem, whether it is hormones or maybe gluten or another type of food allergy or possibly stress overload. First thing to do is to make sure that you give those things to God that you are stressed over everyday and lean on Him and choose to dwell in His shelter. We have a choice, we can choose to fear what might happen or we can give it to God and trust that He will do what is best for us and protect us. If you still struggle with anxiety, you may want to see your doctor or start eliminating different foods that could be causing it as well.

Life can be overwhelming and we live at such a fast pace these days that one thing after the next can just pile up until we don't know which end is up. There are things we bring on ourselves and we usually end up facing the consequences of those, but giving it to God can still affect the outcome of that situation. There were several examples of people in the Old Testament who would get in a mess, like Abraham telling rulers that his wife was his sister, or Jonah in the belly of the Great Fish and even though they made decisions that brought them to where they were God still delivered them so don't lose heart in your situation today. Always ask God for His deliverance and trust Him to do what is best.

We are all facing things that we shouldn't handle on our own and today the choice is yours to either dwell in your terror, mistakes and frustration or to dwell in the shelter of the Most High. Give it all to Him today without holding anything back including your fear of the situation. Ask Him to give you the confidence and faith you need today and just take it one day at a time, knowing His best is yet to come!

Quote:

"The only thing we have to fear is fear itself."
FRANKLIN DELANO ROOSEVELT

~ How Can You Apply This To Your Life Today ~

IN CLOSING

Thank you so much for having taken this 90 Day journey with me! My prayer is truly that your Faith, Hope and Love have grown and that your walk with Him is deeper than it has ever been! He truly loves you more than words can say!

I would like to encourage you to stay in the Word every day and I would love it if you would join me for my daily devotional that you can also find at *www.chocolateandgod.com*.

I would like to leave you with this prayer:

"For this reason I bow my knees before the Father, from whom every family in heaven and on earth is named, that according to the riches of His glory He may grant you to be strengthened with power through His Spirit in your inner being, so that Christ may dwell in your hearts through faith ~ that you, being rooted and grounded in love, may have strength to comprehend with all the saints what is the breadth and length and height and depth, and to know the love of Christ that surpasses knowledge, that you may be filled with all the fullness of God. Now to Him who is able to do far more abundantly than all that we ask or think, according to the power at work within us, to Him be glory in the church and in Christ Jesus throughout all generations, forever and ever. Amen"

God Bless,
Janet Scott

Made in the USA
Monee, IL
23 November 2019